Bill Cherry's Galveston Memories

VanJus Press
Galveston

Cover design and layout by Justine Gilcrease.

Articles are published with the permission of the Galveston County Daily News.

Photos published with permission: *Pop Snow*, Dorothy Snow Lucas; *Chano Rodriguez*, Mrs. Chano Rodriguez; *Charles Kilgore*, Charles Kilgore; *Ardella Connnor*, Frank Defferari; *Sam Farb*, Sam Farb; *Francis Wade*, Galveston County Daily News files; *Utah Carl Beach*, Carl Beach, Jr.; *Bill Latimer*, Bill and Vivian Latimer and Galveston County Daily News file; *G. Martini, A. Martini, Rabbi Henry Cohen,* and *Martini Theater*, Eugene Martini; *George Mitchell portrait*, George Mitchell; *McKee Andrus, Leroy Brown,* and *Jack D. Bushong,* Galveston Rotary Club file; *Kendall, Chic and Nettie,* Ruth Lacquement; *Dwight Cuny, Dr. Peete, George Prader, Wrong Way Corrigan* and *George Roy Clough*, Galveston Rosenberg Library Collection.

ISBN 0-9666438-4-4
Copyright © 2000 by VanJus Press,
1618 -23rd St., Galveston, TX 77550
All Rights Reserved
(409) 762-2333, FAX (409) 762-0411

Dedicated to

William Wallace Cherry (1909-1980), Naomi Speakman Cherry,
Patricia Bowers Cherry, Frederick Wallace Cherry, Judy Fosher
Cherry (1938-1963) and
the love dog, Emmielou Cherry, and
Ethyl the Cat

and especially to

Miss Yvette Rosenthal, Dr. Ralph Eberly, Dr. Ted Colson,
Dr. Leon Breeden, my most valued teachers
and friends for most of my life,

and finally to

Heber Taylor

and

Steve Allen
(1921-2000)

Table of Contents

Foreword ... 1

Nostalgia

1. Her Name Was Louise Bird and She Owned the City's Most Famous Nightclub Ever ... 5
2. Utah Carl Beach with Herbie and the Boys: Galveston's TV Star Pioneers ... 10
3. Wrong Way Corrigan, The Interurban Queen and Slick the Shine Man ... 16
4. What's Important Is Who Plays the Part of Arthur Fonzarelli ... 22
5. Sinatra's Galveston Gig ... 27
6. The Galveston Beach Band ... 30
7. Curly Fox, Miss Texas Ruby, Ozzie and the Boys ... 34
8. Bill Latimer: Island Dad and Son Made Their Home Historically Important ... 37
9. Joe and Jennings Each Try His Hand at Inventing a Better Lawn Mower ... 41
10. Baby Doll Pajamas, Spoolies and Tabu Marked Rites of Passage ... 46
11. John W. Cissne: After Thirty Years, Three of the Four Men Saw True Light for the First Time ... 50

12. Roy Rogers and Sonny Martini: Everyone Mourns the Death of a Good Man   55

13. Bubba Miller: When Galveston's Big Bopper Was Standing, He Looked Like a Capital S   60

14. Rascal McCaskill: The King is Alive and Living in Victoria Texas   64

15. A Lavender 1949 Ford Coupe and a Boy and Girl at the Lagoon were the Root of Envy   67

16. George Prader, D.J.   71

Love

17. At Miss Dorothy's: Arthur and Summer Saw the Midnight Sun   77

18. The Story of Ski, and Antoinette and Jesse Belvin, the Rhythm & Blues Singer   83

19. Smooching Can Make a Boy and Girl Say Things They Don't Mean   89

20. Everyone Needs to Go Into His Cave From Time To Time   94

21. The First Girlfriend, The First Date   97

22. Rose, Curly, the Priest and the Doctor Above the Dime Store   101

23. Andella Conner and the Rubaiyat of Omar Khayyam   107

24. When George's Courage Took Him to His First Dance Ever, He Met Mary — 111

25. Tina, Sammy and Nat "King" Cole's "That Sunday, That Summer" — 116

Humor

26. The Elements of Style — 123

27. 1909: Young Men's Progressive Association Opens Model Laundry — 129

28. Galveston's Twin Foondinis, the Inspiration for Las Vegas' Siegfried and Roy? — 134

29. It Took a Fire at the Laundromat for the World to Learn Crawford's Secret — 138

30. Champ's European Shopping Spree Turned Out to Be a Mistake — 142

31. Homer Sechtuals — 147

32. Blackie's New Rug and Veralee's Solution to the Problem — 152

33. Nettie Always Shot Them in the Neck — 155

34. Joe Pajucie, His Red Cadillac Convertible and the Four Cheap-Looking Girls — 159

35. George Mitchell: The Horatio Alger "Strive and Succeed" Award — 163

36. The Botched Texas Ranger Raid — 167

History

37. Pop Snow — 175

38. Dr. Peete and the Home He Designed to Save His Family — 179

39. Battle of Galveston: John Magruder Was a "Give Me Liberty or Give Me Death" Kind of a Guy — 183

40. How Galveston Saved Itself from Self-Destruction in 1901 — 189

41. In 1916, A New Hobby of Stamp Collecting Uncovered His Father's Secret Life — 194

42. Galveston — 199

43. In 1889, A. Martini Was a Poor Immigrant. In 1937, He Was the Wealthiest Italian in Texas — 204

44. Son of Spanish Nobleman, Designed Studio Lounge and Balinese Room — 209

Hurricanes

45. The Surprise Ending to a Carriage Ride — 217

46. Hurricane Carla: Event That Marked the Island's New Beginning — 221

Religion

47. Recounting His First Memory of His Life on Earth — 229

48. School Prayer: Prior to 1963 Prayer Brought Educators a Different Challenge — 234

Business

49. The Story of Sam's Galveston Gold Mine — 241

50. Jim Woodall's Contributions to the Island and Its People Live After Him — 244

51. A Lesson to the Man Who Tried to Call the Banker a Crook — 248

52. The Purity Ice Cream Factory and the Ten O'Clock Valve — 252

53. Y2K Has Little on 1960 — 255

Galveston Characters

54. 1947: Galveston Hosts National Happy Hermits Political Convention — 261

55. Monk and the Bartender Set the Clock Back for the Alibi — 266

56. When Safety Santa Arrived at Perusina's, Only McCoy Farqua was Caught by Surprise — 270

Memories

57. Friends Archie Crow and Leroy Brown Got Together One Last Time — 277

58. David Goodbar — 281

59. Johnny's Part in a Class Act Comes to an End — 285

60. Frank Sinatra Should Have Picked Chano Rodriguez — 288

Forewond

The year was 1940. World War II was going on in Europe and three important military installations were on Galveston Island. Since just prior to the Civil War, Galveston had been one of the US's most important ports, and a lot of families had set up businesses here because of it.

By 1940, many millions had been earned and spent on glamourous Galveston Island.

And just like history shows, when lots of money comes to a seaport town, up sprouts demographics comprised of society folk and poor folk, and they immediately surround themselves with light vice—open gambling, prostitution, and wise guys running rampant. That was the Galveston where I was born in 1940.

But the world was put on hold throughout the 40s as the boys fought overseas and earned paychecks which were far less than a hundred bucks a month. Their young wives and their children were forced to move back home with their parents. Construction of new houses stopped, and as far as Galveston was concerned anyway, life all but stood still until the early 50s.

When I played with my friends, their grandparents, great-grandparents and aunts and uncles wove for us the stories of Galveston's past. They even told us what it was like to have survived the terrible 1900 Storm, for many of them had. All are the stories that were not written before I began putting them down. Adddded to these stories are the tales that'll let you know what it was like growing up and living on the Island through the 1960s. You'll love these stories.

I was educated in the Galveston public schools, then at Tulane University and North Texas State University. In real life I became a commerical real-estate broker, a profession that was good to me throughout my thirty-five year career. But in my mind's eye I chose to see myself as a jazz pianist and author.

Early retirement manifested new professions—piano tuning and writer—and that earned me a place amongst "Galveston Characters." When locals speak, I can proudly report that I am now included with the other characters like Harry the Hat, Christie "the Beachcomber" Mitchell, Safety Santa, Joe Pajucie and Clay Pigeon Dunahee.

For me, life on Galveston Island has been good.

Nostalgia

Her Name Was Louise Bird and She Owned the City's Most Famous Nightclub Ever

Even though more than forty years have passed, few of us who were around here then will ever forgive those who squashed our town's personality and took away its reason for being.

There is no way anyone can look at the island's newspapers from the 30s through the early 60s, compare them to those of today, and say Galveston is better off. Galveston is very obviously far less prosperous.

But don't take my word for it. Go to the Rosenberg Library's Galveston and Texas History Center, and look through any issues of "The Galveston Daily News" or the "Galveston Tribune" of that era, then decide for yourself.

While there have been many stories advanced as to why Galveston was forced to change, the most interesting one centers around a prominent and big wig physician at UTMB who was also a deacon in his church. According to the stories, he went to the Balinese Room one night, the first time he'd ever been there, and blew some serious bucks while showing off for some "visiting firemen" he was trying to recruit for the school. The next morning on reflection, he became a sore loser—one sore enough to want to retaliate.

He called his friends at the capitol in Austin for help. "You'll have to close up Galveston," he said. The reason he presented for them doing that was so that he would no longer get resistance when he was trying to employ staff for his department at the university. Most people don't want to live and raise their families in a town like Galveston, he claimed. The doctor apparently inadvertently overlooked mentioning anything about his own personal losses the night before at the Balinese.

His friends in the state government said they would back the idea of closing the illegal operations in Galveston, for after all, election time was coming, but there'd have to be someone other than the doctor making the demands.

The doctor solicited the help of his old friend, the editor of the Texas City Sun, Silas Ragsdale. Ragsdale took the reigns and began the beating death of the foe in November 1951. Dr. Harold Fickett, pastor of Galveston's First Baptist Church, became the movement's passionate orator.

One of the most beautiful women, in fact I'll go so far as to say the most beautiful woman, who ever graced the shores of this island was the matriarch of the Galveston nightclub scene, Louise Bird.

In the early 1930s, she was still Louise McComb, and was a twenty-five-year-old Ft. Worth-born beauty who had moved here with her family. The McComb family lived at 2314 Avenue Q.

Louise took a job as a cashier at the Snug Harbor Café. Shortly thereafter, she married a musician, Samuel E. Bird.

Around the corner from the Snug Harbor, behind the Hotel Buccaneer, were Milton Wilkenfleld's Turkish bath with an alleged cat house renter upstairs, Willie Wisko's Beach Amusement Parlor, James Reese's Henry's Grill, James Smith's James' Beauty Salon, Irving "Fuzzy" Hobbit's beer joint and the Buccaneer Garage, which Hobbit also ran.

When the Buccaneer Hotel's management gave Hobbit an ultimatum, the beer joint or his job at the garage, the beer joint went out of business. With the backing of a local soft drink bottler whom she had met at the Snug Harbor, Louise Bird rented the building and it became the Pirate Club. That was in 1939. And that was the beginning of the most famous one of the long-lasting nightclubs Galveston ever had. About that time, Louise and Sam Bird divorced.

For the next twenty years, the stars that played Galveston used the Pirate Club as their home base. Visitors went there to rub elbows with them, just as tourists and townspeople did at the Brown Derby in Hollywood. Oftentimes, those stars would do an impromptu show for the customers of the Pirate Club.

The Pirate Club was where bandleader-pianist Jack Fina tried out for the first time his "Bumble Boogie," his famous take-off on the classical piece by Rimsky-Korsakov, "Flight of the Bumble Bee."

It was where Myron Cohen, Jack Benny, Phil Harris, Red Buttons, Larry Storch, Gracie Allen, and

Peter Lind Hayes and Mary Healy told their stories. It was where Frank Sinatra, Diana Lynn, Ella Fitzgerald, Tony Martin, Mel Torme and Alice Faye sang, and it was where Fred Astaire danced.

If you got there after the stars had stopped coming to Galveston, you knew the legend of the Pirate Club was true because the walls in the bar were graced by nearly a hundred signed 8 1/2 x 11 publicity photos of them.

About 1960, the National Hotel chain bought the entire block, and the buildings that housed the Pirate Club and its neighbors were torn down. Louise Bird moved her business to 2301 Avenue Q, where Otis Skains' famous Rod and Gun Club had been. Just before then, Skains had sold his business to Colony Club's owner Lee Woodson's wife, Donna, and she had moved it downtown.

Since the old Rod and Gun Club building was already equipped with a kitchen and dining room, Bird added food to the Pirate Club's bill of fare, and along with the food came Galveston's famous food waiter, Francis Wade. Known to customers as "Wade," he always referred to his customers as "papa" and himself in the third person as "papa" as well.

("Good evening, Papa. Is Papa going to have his usual? Excuse me while Papa goes and gets it from the bar," is a paragraph in Wade-speak.)

Also Skains' famous cook, a heavyset woman named "Oscar," stayed on when the location became the Pirate Club. Norris Ellis, the club's most famous bartender, came with Bird from the old club.

Galveston Memories

The Pirate Club remained at 23d and Avenue Q until 1966 when it then moved to 1808 Avenue P, the site of the former Joila's Sidewalk Café and French Door Club, that had been owned by another Galveston beauty, Joila Walker.

By 1970, Bird was in poor health and her daughter Betty Jean took over the Pirate Club's reigns. She moved it to 2015 Postoffice where it subsequently breathed its dying breath.

Louise Bird, 72, died September 27 1977; Norris Ellis, 58, died June 5, 1983; and Francis Wade, 79, died February 1994. The Pirate Club along with the Island, in both their elegant and legendary formats, had died years before.

Francis Wade

Utah Carl Beach with Herbie and the Boys: Galveston's TV Star Pioneers

'm just the wanderer of the wasteland
Ridin' along and thinkin' 'bout days gone by.
And when I'm feelin' kinda lonesome,
I sing this cowboy lullaby.

When I was young
I used to be
A high falutin', rootin'-tootin', son of a gun
Up in Wyomin'....

are the words to his theme song, a song everyone is sure he didn't write, but a song whose author no reference source I checked was able to name. Nevertheless, all agree it was Carl Jared Beach who made this tune famous. Without his rendition, few would have ever heard it.

He was born on an Indian reservation in Bartlesville, Oklahoma, and he was half-Cherokee and half-Irish. He grew up in Coffeyville, Kansas, and entertained on fifty-six radio stations as he crossed the country looking for places that would book him. Once he was a strolling cowboy guitarist in the casino at Las Vegas' Last Frontier Hotel. But that was in the early 40s, when Las

Vegas was a nowhere place, and Galveston was "King of the Mountain."

His career as a troubadour started when he went to a county fair in Coffeyville the year after he had bought his first guitar for $3.00 on the installment plan. While at the fair, he and his friends decided to get their fortunes told.

Beach said in 1959, "The first thing the fortune teller said to me was, 'I see you play the guitar and sing. You've got a nice radio station here. Now you go up there and go to work for them.' It was the depression, jobs were hard to find, and I was only 12 years old. Well, I went that Saturday morning to KGGF, and by golly, they put me on the air the same morning."

It was during the Las Vegas stint the he married Juanita Mavers. While he had his Coffeyville radio program, she had sent him a number of postcard requests to play her favorite tunes on the air, signing them "Juanita."

A few months before he left for Las Vegas, Beach was playing at a Coffeyville dance. He was introduced to "a pretty brunette with liquid-blue, dreamy eyes. We started dancing and she looked up at me and said, 'I'm Juanita.' Before the night was over, I knew she was the one."

Later Beach was playing a few numbers as a guest artist on a Mutual Broadcasting Network program called "Hymns of All Churches." The first song he sang was an old cowboy song titled "Utah Carl's Last Ride." It was at that moment that for the heck of it the program's announcer began addressing Beach as "Utah Carl." The name stuck.

And while it's true that Utah Carl Beach was once a real six-foot-six cowboy, punching cattle for nearly five years, if he ever so much as went to the state of Utah, he was just passing through. Nevertheless, for the remainder of his career as an entertainer, which spanned forty-three years, "Utah" was the prefix to "Carl."

In 1945, when the Las Vegas engagement was over, Utah Carl moved his family to Galveston. He was signed on for a regular daily program at radio station KLUF, along with the station's other western program, "Boots Darr and Her Guitar."

In the evenings, he and his band entertained at various taverns in Galveston, like the Westwego, the Hurricane Club, and Fatty Owen's Anchor Club.

When he later reminisced about those days, he said, "Some of the things I've seen would stand your hair up—like in a night club, I'd be singing and a couple of guys would get in a knife fight and get killed right in front of my eyes. Many a night I've torn the doors off places getting out of there."

Utah Carl began his career in television the day television began its career in Galveston. It was in 1953. He was awakened by the police from an afternoon nap and rushed to the new studios of the area's CBS affiliate, KGUL-TV, just north of where Tom's Thumb Nursery is today. Its address was 11 Video Lane.

Movie actor Jimmy Stewart was one of the owners

of the new station, and he was in Galveston to emcee the opening along with Paul Taft, who was the station's president. The next thing on the program was to have been a Jimmy Stewart movie. When the cue was given the projectionist, he pulled the projector's switch, and nothing happened.

Someone in the audience of dignitaries suggested Utah Carl could fill the time, and Stewart sent the police to get him. He played a twenty-five-minute impromptu set. When it was over, and the next act came in, Stewart and Taft took Utah Carl into the office, and signed him as a permanent member of the station's staff.

For the next fourteen years, Utah Carl with "Herbie and the boys" had a regular television show. For most of those years, it was sponsored by Gulf Coast Furniture Warehouse in Alvin, run by his friend Hob Holcomb. On weekends when the furniture company's customers came to shop, just like Utah Carl had promised them on the air, he and his band were performing on a stage that was set up in the parking lot.

In the late 1950s, Utah Carl released on records two of his compositions—"Daddy's Little King" and "The Man in the Moon." The hoopla for the releases was a Western jamboree that, along with Utah Carl, featured Ernest Tubb, Hank Snow, the Texas Troubadours and others. The shows were held at Galveston's City Auditorium and along with a clambake at Houston's Buff Stadium.

Two of the staffers at KGUL-TV took a break from their duties at the station to play on the two records. Frank Incaprera, who ran the station's film room, was featured on trumpet, and Pat Bradley, one of KGUL's floor directors, played drums. Others were Russell Reed, piano, and George Achord, electric guitar.

Other tunes Utah Carl wrote and recorded for Nashville's Bullet Recording Co. were "It's No, My Darling," "Memories by My Fireside," and "Treasured Memories."

For most of his performing years in Galveston, Utah Carl's band featured Herbie Treece, steel guitar; Fidlo Ericksen, guitar; and Cecil Bowman, bass. Others who frequently played with his band were Don Cathy, Phil Parr, George Champion, Wiley Barkdull, Don Brewer and Clem Cajaura.

During the last 15 years of his life, Utah Carl was an agent for Prudential Insurance Co.'s Galveston office, and was enormously successful. He was Leader of the Million-Dollar Roundtable, and, in fact, its executive vice president in 1966. Utah Carl died of carcinoma of the lung at St. Mary's Hospital at 6 a.m. on Saturday, September 24, 1977. He was 57.

On Monday, just before his 10:15 a.m. funeral mass at St. Mary's Cathedral, on a whim, Fidlo Ericksen borrowed instruments from Ginsberg's Music Center across the street, and Utah Carl's band set-up in the cathedral's loft and played one last time. The final tune before Fr. Paul Chovonec began the service was appropriately "Utah Carl's Last Ride."

> *My friend, you ask the question,*
> *Why I'm so sad and still*
> *Why my brow is always darkened*
> *Like a cloud upon the hill*

*There's a grave, without a headstone
Without a date or name
In silence sleeps my comrade
In the land from which I came*

*Long we had ridden together
We had ridden side by side
I wept when Utah died.*

Surviving Utah Carl were his wife, Juanita; son, Carl, Jr. and his wife, Pat; daughter, Sandra Pfundstein and her husband, Frank; grandchildren, Carl Beach III, Tracy Nemetz, Frank Pfundstein, IV, Troy Pfundstein; great grandchildren, David and Lauren Nemetz and Stewart and Spencer Pfundstein; and sister-in-law, Roberta Beach.

Fans of Utah Carl will remember that as a child, Carl, Jr. stood by his dad during the television shows, the opening shot being the right boot of each, patting time to the show's theme song. Hand carved on one boot was Utah Carl. On the other was Utah Carl, Jr.

Utah Carl Beach

I am deeply grateful to Pat Beach, Utah Carl's most loyal fan, for her enormous assistance in gathering for me the facts for this story, and the contributions of Juanita Beach, Roberta Beach, Betty Ericksen, Jack Solari, Nancy McKenney, Burt Lindsey, G.R. Richard, F.W. Cherry, Raymond Haak, Harry Levy, III and others.

Wrong Way Corrigan, The Interurban Queen and Slick the Shine Man

There was a small and weathered bronze plaque just to the left side of the entrance that took you to the upstairs of the Gill Building. It noted that Douglas "Wrong Way" Corrigan had been born there in 1907.

The Gill building stood on the southeast corner of 21st and Market streets, and was the building whose architecture featured the multitude of bay windows that made it the anomaly among the iron-front buildings that surrounded it.

In his late teens, after he had left Galveston for California, Corrigan took a job in a San Diego airplane factory. In fact, he worked on the aircraft that Charles Lindberg used in 1927, to solo across the Atlantic. That must have given Corrigan his inspiration.

Because in 1938, he applied to aviation officials to allow him to solo across the Atlantic in a used plane he had bought for $310. There was no reason to believe Corrigan could accomplish that feat, especially in that airplane, so the Bureau of Air Commerce denied permission.

He then asked if he could fly his plane back to California, and that petition was granted.

So Corrigan took off on July 17, 1938, and twenty-eight hours later, after having gotten nowhere near California, landed in Ireland. When the officials found out, they were furious.

Corrigan tried to gloss over his transgression by insisting he had made an understandable mistake. He claimed that his compass froze, and it, therefore, misdirected him to Ireland rather than to California. "When I came down through the clouds, I noticed I had been reading the compass needle backward," he explained. "Then I landed, and I knew I was somewhere other than California. This place was greener and some of the houses had hay roofs." It was a story he would stick to with the remainder of his life.

He became an instant celebrity, was nicknamed "Wrong Way" and was given a New York Wall Street ticker-tape parade when he got back to the states. Then Galveston Mayor Adrian Levy honored him here with a parade.

Because of Corrigan's instant, strong celebrity status, rather than take away his license and subject itself to public outrage and political disdain, the Bureau of Air Commerce gave him a five-day suspension. Later he flew for the Army in World War II, and starred in a Hollywood feature, "The Flying Irishman."

About the time Corrigan was preparing for what was to be that historic flight, another Galvestonian, Chris

Tellefson, decided to move his business from 21st and Winnie streets to the downstairs of the Gill building.

Even though by then he had been in business for 10 years, Tellefson was better known for the barbecued shrimp and oysters he cooked for friends. In 1945, he said that the secrets for his acclaimed recipes were twofold: he only used shrimp and oysters from R.S. Maceo's seafood market, and his "spit fires were made from driftwood logs laid in a hole dug in the beach's sand."

Tellefson was also a champion story teller. He attributed that talent to his "photographic mind's ability to remember facts and details." But what had been the main reasons for Tellefson's notoriety in Galveston soon were to change.

While H.P. Nettleton had been an excellent printing engraver for Clark and Courts, it was his avocation for which he was best known. Nettleton was a superb taxidermist.

He had collected and mounted almost every imaginable specimen of marine, animal and bird life. It was because of Nettleton that Tellefson had decided to move his business to the Gill building. You see, Nettleton had died, and Tellefson had purchased the entire collection from Nettleton's widow.

Tellefson wanted that collection to become the basis of a free museum he would install as the "loss-leader" in the new and bigger location of the Interurban Queen Cigar and Newsstand, which he owned with his partner, Tom McKenna. In addition to the stuffed wild life, they continued to add curios to the collection until there were more than 7,000 items on display.

For example, there you could see the second largest pair of Texas longhorns in the world. The horns were slightly more than seven feet from end to end. And, of course, there was the frog that Tellefson had bought from the famous Dick Wick Hall Saloon in Salome, Arizona. The frog's claim to fame was that it couldn't swim. Since it was both dead and stuffed, by the time it reached the Interurban Queen Cigar and Newsstand, that point was moot.

The most valuable piece was a family tree that someone had made. It traced the important families of the world from Adam and Eve, through the Stone Age, the Ice Age, and the other great historic events, to the year of 1881. Tellefson and McKenna had bought the family tree from the estate of a former Galveston mayor.

On the west wall was a shark's mouth with a huge board below it. Tellefson claimed that when the shark was caught, the board was found lodged in its stomach. Although that story didn't seem likely, no one seemed willing to contest it.

There were land grants signed by former U.S. presidents, John Quincy Adams, James Monroe and Andrew Jackson. There was an entire area dedicated to sports memorabilia, including the autographs of baseball great Ty Cobb, champion fighter Jess Willard, famous black boxer Jack Johnson, and sailboat regatta enthusiast Sir Thomas Lipton.

Every city bus that traveled the island in those days

stopped on the west or east side of 21st and Market streets. It was hard for any child or adult to get off at the bus stop and not find a reason to go into the Interurban Queen. Pinball and slot machines lined the otherwise unused walls; white porcelain cuspidors were at the foot of each. Cigar and cigarette smoke of both the past and the present hovered with the smell of the paper and the ink of the sleazy, like the "Police Gazette," and the hauteur, like the "Saturday Review of Literature." And there were more comic books there than any child could possibly imagine.

But as Tellefson had anticipated, it was the museum of curios that was the Interurban Queen's true attraction.

On the alley corner of the Gill building, next to the newsstand, was a shoe shine parlor that, while it had many proprietors over the years, the operator had always gone by the moniker, "Slick." In addition to shining shoes, the last proprietor who used the named "Slick" sold records, mostly rhythm and blues.

It was just before Christmas in 1949. The movie cowboy Gene Autry had just released his "Rudolph the Red Nose Raindeer," and for some reason Slick decided to stock the record. While Slick was shining shoes, a small loudspeaker above the front door to the shine parlor played Christmas music.

One night, after the shine parlor had closed and the lights had been turned out, Autry's song began repeating itself over the loudspeaker. A couple of hours passed. It continued. People at the bus stop began complaining to Tellefson. Tellefson finally told the beat cop who had come in for a package of Sano cigarettes.

The policeman called Tom Sedgwick, a locksmith known as the "Mayor of 22nd Street," to pick the shine parlor's lock so the cop could get in to turn off the record changer. That's when they discovered Slick with his throat slit, lying face-up on his cot in the back of the shine parlor where he lived. He had been the victim of a jealous husband. From then on, when Tellefson was telling stories about the characters of the Gill building, he always called Slick "Wrong Way Slick."

Shortly thereafter, Tellefson and McKenna moved the Interurban Queen Cigar and Newsstand to 2019 Market St. It was sold ten years later to Victor Hayes, who owned it briefly, then sold it to Vincent Gina. Gina operated it for about thirty more years. It was closed for good a few years back when Gina passed away.

As for the Gill building, it was judged to be beyond repair and torn down. Later the adjacent buildings were as well. Today the entire half block is a parking lot. One wag said that if Tellefson were alive, he would probably call it the "Wrong Way Preservation Park and Lock."

Wrong Way Corrigan

What's Important Is Who Plays the Part of Arthur Fonzarelli

The movie about being a teenager in the early 60s, "American Graffiti," cost less than a million bucks to produce, but audiences everywhere loved it and it made its creator, Gene Lucas, a rich man and an icon.

In fact, "American Graffiti" was the basis for a television sitcom, "Happy Days," which had a ten-year, 255-show, prime time run and it continues in syndication.

But what many don't know and others choose to forget is that "Happy Days" almost laid a big egg, and it would have, had the character of Arthur Fonzarelli not later been added to the show.

In "American Graffiti," John Milner had a customized chopped coupe, and was a high school dropout whose only ambition was being able to have the fastest car in town. As a person, he was a loser and all of those around him knew it. He was no one's role model.

The only memorable words John Milner uttered throughout the entire show were, "Rock 'n roll died with Buddy Holly."

Galveston Memories

In the first few episodes of "Happy Days" there was no Arthur Fonzarelli. Then he was introduced to prop up the show. In the original, "The Fonz" was modeled after Milner—Fonzie was a loser, a high school dropout.

But with the introduction of the Fonzie character, "Happy Days" still didn't produce acceptable ratings. The writers knew that they would have to make more changes if the show was to survive. It was then that they made a profound decision. They reinvented Fonzie. This time he was a street kid, albeit a high school dropout, but he had successfully figured out life on his own.

The new Arthur Fonzarelli was revered by his peers and loved by the grown-ups. He was moral and always dished out the right advice. He was the role model,

Victor Damiani

although incongruously he was one in jeans, tee shirt, leather jacket and duck tails—visually he was the model of a rebel. The revised Fonzie character saved "Happy Days."

About two years ago, my friend Vic's wife, Judy, threw a sixtieth birthday party for him, and she made sure that his old friends from high school were there. Many of us hadn't seen each other in a long time, and it had been almost forty years since we had all been together.

As we visited, we learned that each of us had gotten college degrees, had been reasonably successful in our professions, had kept our noses clean, and had survived almost as many "downs" as we had had "ups."

All of this information came from the discussion the circle of old friends had as they stood near Vic and Judy's fireplace. It was also then, as we retold the stories that recounted our past as friends, that we realized for the first time in our nearly forty-five-year history, that Vic had been our Fonzie. That revelation was profound to every one of us. Not one of us had realized it prior to that moment.

A widowed aunt and a spinster cousin had raised Vic. In their house was a great deal of love, but very little money. Even as a small child he had to work if he was to have the essentials. Between the ages of twelve and eighteen he had been a bowling-alley pin boy, a bus boy and runner for a bingo parlor, and an ambulance attendant for a funeral home.

Most of the things about life, Vic had figured out by himself, and, for the most part, he had figured them out correctly. He shared his takes on life with us.

"You want a car? Your family doesn't owe you a car. Get a job, earn the money and buy your own," he said.

"You'll never save enough money to buy a car unless you have a systematic savings plan. To do that, you'll need a savings account at the bank. I'll take you to the bank so you can open your account."

"All of us have jobs, and we could all use help during our individual busy times. What we need to do is to help each other. When it's time to make and deliver homecoming mum corsages, we'll help J.E. at Elbert's Flower Shop. On Fridays we'll help Artie deliver the liquor and cigarettes to the nightclubs for his daddy. When we have a big funeral at Malloy's, you guys can help people find the guest register and stiff," Vic taught us.

"How're you coming with saving up for your car? Have you opened a checking account yet? You've got to have a checking account when you go to buy your car. You transfer just the right amount of money from your savings account to your checking account, then you write the man a check for your car. Come on, I'll take you down to the bank. We can cruise the stores while we're down there."

"Miss Coldwell is an excellent teacher. It must be something you're doing wrong. Go see Mr. Graham. He'll help you and Miss Coldwell resolve your differences. If that doesn't work, maybe Mr. Morton will let you transfer to Mrs. Pfeiffer's class. She's a great teacher and she's pretty. She's Freda and Harriet's mother, you know. I had her last year."

"I'll be at church at First Pres tomorrow because it's Sunday. If you're not going to your church, you can go with me. I'll pick you up."

Because he was a year or so older than the rest of us, Vic was always the one who first explored the unknown and then paved the way for us. He was the first to get a permanent job, the first to marry, the first to have children and the first to feel the pains brought by divorce.

He was the first to buy a home, the first to move from the island and the first to begin having the health problems that come congruently with each age milestone. He was the first of us to fund the education of a child and the first to be there for a sick and obviously dying parent.

As before, he was there to help us when those issues entered our lives and demanded our immediate and correct decision. After all, he had been there.

So at Vic's sixtieth birthday party, in one of the small groups, a commercial real-estate broker, a well-known psychiatrist, a piano tuner and a charitable foundation executive and attorney, contemporaneously got the revelation it took them nearly forty years to discover: It may not be as important who your parents are as it is who you pick to be Fonzie.

Vic's sixtieth Birthday Party. Left to right: E. Douglas McLeod, JD; Ward McReynolds, MD; Bill Cherry; Jasper E. Tramonte; Victor J. Damiani

Sinatra's Galveston Gig

The Speedway Cafe was a glorified two-bit diner on 22nd Street just behind an enormous wood-framed rollercoaster called the Mountain Speedway, the Buccaneer Hotel, and the Beach Amusement Parlor which was called Willie Wisko's Bingo by locals. Above the bingo was Milton's Turkish Bath.

We're talking about 1950.

Fifty miles away the king of hotels was the Shamrock owned by legendary oilman Glenn McCarthy. Its plush and famous nightclub was the Cork Club, and while top stars frequently appeared there and at the neighboring Tidelands Club, as you might suspect down-and-out has-beens did too.

In 1950, Frank Sinatra, all but broke, worked his way into a two week engagement at the Cork Club, not as a star but as a has been. Houston newspapers reported that his wife, Ava Gardner, was with him, but as the facts of their deteriorating life together were later revealed, it is doubtful she was. It's for certain nobody remembers seeing her ringside.

When his stay in Houston was over, there was no immediate booking to follow, so Sinatra came to Galveston to see if he might find work at one of the Maceo night spots, hopefully the Balinese, but if need be, he'd take the small, more intimate and lesser known Studio Lounge which was where the Bank of America building stands today.

The money he had earned at the Cork Club was needed to pay past due bills, so he rented a small room in a $2 per night, off-the-beach fleabag hotel and sang at the Balinese Room, not as the headliner but as a featured attraction with the band. Supper came with his gig, but breakfast and lunch came as handouts at the Speedway Cafe which was owned by Biaggio De Andrea.

If you were at Louise Bird's Pirate Club in the wee hours, you could hear Sinatra as he and pianist Al Pliner and Pliner's sidemen jammed there. Tips were accepted.

Vic Damiani, singer Kate Martelli's cousin, was about twelve years old then, and worked as a busboy at Wisko's Bingo. He remembers Sinatra being in and out of the parlor with little notice from the players. Occasionally one of the grandmothers, cigarette drooping from her lips, would tip Sinatra if he would join her in a photo to show her friends back home. But even that, Damiani says, didn't qualify as fanfare.

But within two years of his Galveston gig, Sinatra was back on top, recreating himself this time as a dramatic star in the movie "From Here to Eternity." He never forgot his Galveston days, and especially the benevolence shown him by Biaggio De Andrea and his Speedway Cafe.

Galveston Memories

When John F. Kennedy asked Sinatra whom he would like to see on the inaugration list of invitees, along with others, Sinatra, who had campaigned heavily for Kennedy, named his friends at the Speedway Cafe, and invitations were sent them.

Until the Speedway closed, one of those invitations was still casually thumb tacked to the wall behind the lunch counter for all to see.

Left to right: Anthony Fertitta, Jimmy Van Heusen, Frank Sinatra and Sam Maceo at the Balinese Room (photo from Galveston Isle Magazine, March 1950)

The Galveston Beach Band

The Galveston Beach Band celebrated its seventieth anniversary in 1998 with its usual summer Tuesday night concert in the park that's sandwiched between Ashton Villa and the Rosenberg Library.

Frank and Hazel Incaprera have been a part of that band, and we, who are old time Galvestonians, have been a part of its audience for so many years that we're family. And you know how it is with a family celebration. Everybody brings food to be shared by all. And the kids and the grand kids come, and great grandma and great grandpa get there, even if its with the assistance of a wheelchair and a nurse.

It's still the case on summer Tuesday nights at 7:30, and if you want to for just one night relive something of the Galveston's past I write about, that's your chance. After all, Frank and Hazel's dance band played at every glitzy night spot that was on this island, at one time or another, in addition to their commitment to the Galveston Beach Band.

Each program will predictably be its usual hodgepodge. Some big band dance numbers, a few Sousa marches, as well as one or two specialty numbers that I guess I'd be tired of hearing if Frank and Hazel weren't having such a good time as a result of including them. A couple of kids will get up and do a routine they could easily also do on Don Mahoney's TV talent show if this were 1954.

Hazel will sing in a Kenton's June Christy like style, and Frank will take a trumpet solo or two, amazing those who know how this all works that his chops can still make a horn sound like that.

Then about midway through the program there'll be the Don McNeil's Breakfast Club style march. There is no way you can't find this the highlight of the program. The band strikes up the Mickey Mouse theme song at which time the kids, the parents, the friends and usually a couple of dogs, line up, most with American flags, and begin a march up and down the aisles. No one is self-conscious. No one is embarrassed.

And you know who the parade marshal will be. It'll be old Frank, who week after week has more fun being in the parade than any of the other participants. Hazel will be banging on the bass drum while delighting in watching pied piper Frank and his followers. And believe me, they'll be having one whale of a good time themselves.

Traditionally the audience stands throughout the zillion verses of the song, clapping to keep time, and then the whole thing ends up on the steps at the stage and reforms itself, this time in several horizontal lines.

At that point, Frank always says, "Ladies and Gentlemen, please remain standing for our National

Anthem!" The audience now facing at least seventy-five of God's American children, and almost that many American Flags, sings the "Star Spangled Banner."

At this point my elderly mother usually gets tears in her eyes, and it isn't hard to know why. Galveston families have done this activity so many times together in the past that it is a true tradition. Frank's own father, another Frank Incaprera, led this band for many years before him.

Relatives and friends who once were here with us, no longer are, having moved elsewhere, with a substantial portion having relocated to that special "elsewhere" we call heaven where my mother's only husband, the man who was my father, has now been for twenty years.

The Galveston Beach Band is comprised of about twenty-five professional musicians from throughout Galveston and Harris counties. Almost all are school-band directors, so you rarely hear sour notes, and when you do, let me clear this up for you right now. It is proper Galveston Beach Band audience etiquette to imagine it didn't happen at all. "If you think you heard a wrong note, I'll assure you either you didn't, or it was the result of a misprint in the sheet music," you are suppose to say to your neighbor while he nods in agreement.

But the very best part of these concerts is watching Frank and Hazel enjoy themselves as much as they do. The only way I can describe this is by comparing it to another story.

Sherwood Brown was a lawyer here of great intellect. Frequently Sherwood would tell a story that amused him. His stories were always so convoluted it was hard to see what amused him. But he would get so tickled as he told them, that everyone loved to hear a Sherwood tale because it brought him such delight telling it.

Well, that's pretty much what happens with Hazel and Frank. They enjoy the Galveston Beach Band concerts so much themselves, that the audience likes it because they do.

So, there we have it. The Galveston Beach Band Concert under the stars, summer Tuesday nights, beginning at 7:30. Be prepared to be in the parade, and don't forget your camera.

And tell me that either Hazel or Frank look like they are anywhere near old enough to have been married for over fifty years.

Curly Fox, Miss Texas Ruby, Ozzie and the Boys

Milton Berle celebrated his nintieth birthday. Within what seemed to be only a handful of moments thereafter, Howdy Doody lost his best friend Buffalo Bob. To most of the U.S. they were the most beloved of the original television performers, but not here.

To us it was Curly Fox and Miss Texas Ruby with their sidemen Ozzie, Alvie and Dean, all brought to us at seven on Friday nights, later on Saturday nights, by the only television channel in Houston at the time, KPRC, Channel 2.

Curly played the fiddle and Texas Ruby sang. It was a country music format with at least one old time gospel tune added in. Miss Texas Ruby always did that in front of a fake stained glass window. She appeared deeply religious.

Ozzie usually soloed at least one number on his steel guitar. He had blond hair with a curl hanging down on his forehead and a goofy grin.

Alvie played guitar, and Dean the bass. Dick

Gottlieb, with his booming voice, announced, and a radio announcer named Bob Gordon played a Mexican foil named Poncho.

Until Curly Fox and Texas Ruby entered the Houston scene, Finger Furniture was, for the most part, a nowhere, nobody family-owned store merchandising to those of Houston's lower economic populace. When they started sponsoring the Curly Fox and Texas Ruby program, all of that changed, and the Finger family pocketbooks grew exponentially.

For years the story has circulated that Curly and Ruby met in prison, that Ruby was in there for killing her husband, and that Curly had been a bank robber. None of that is true. Here's the scoop.

Ruby was the sister of radio cowboy Tex Owens, and she was born in 1908 and raised on a ranch in Wise County near Decatur. Curly's name was Arnim Fox, and he was from Graysville, Tennessee. His barber father taught him to play the fiddle. He was two years younger than Ruby.

Curly and Ruby met while appearing on the Grand Ole Opry in 1937. Within a short time they married and had two daughters. In the early 40s they became regulars on a radio station in Cincinnati, replacing Doris Day who was joining the Les Brown Orchestra for Bob Hope's radio and road show.

They hit pay dirt when they got to Houston in 1948, first doing a radio program for KPRC-AM, and then adding their weekly television program in 1950. Their broadcasting fame made them popular and well-paid dance hall entertainers.

Galveston Memories

Ruby's health began to fail, so in 1960 they moved back to Nashville so that Texas Ruby could retire, and Curly could rejoin the Grand Ole Opry.

On the night of March 29, 1963, while Curly was performing at the Opry, the Fox's house trailer caught fire, and Miss Texas Ruby burned to death.

Curly moved to Chicago to retire and live with one of his daughters. Restless to perform again, he went back to his hometown of Graysville, this time lived with an older sister, and worked with bluegrass bands until his death, November 12, 1995.

There is one CD available of Curly's music, none of Texas Ruby's. Called, "Champion Fiddler Curly Fox—18 Old-time Country Favorites," it quickly provides the appropriate background music for reminiscing of a simpler time on the gulf coast.

All you have to do is close your eyes and look into your memory's photo album. There you'll find you and your family watching television for the first time, and it's more than fifty years ago.

Bill Latimer: Island Dad and Son Made Their Home Historically Important

In the 1950s, Galveston teenage boys were not impressed with the Henry Rosenberg statue in front of the library or the Texas Heroes' Monument at 25th and Broadway. This lack of enthusiasm perplexed their history teachers, Blanche Saunders and Catherine Redmond.

To make matters worse, going on a field trip to see the San Jacinto Monument in Houston was viewed by the boys as penance for the stopover afterwards at the San Jacinto Inn, where the bill of fare was "all you can eat" fried chicken and boiled shrimp.

No, the boys felt that the important history was that which was being made in a family's garage at 1310 Bowie. And the basic inspiration for that history in the making should be credited to a Lithuanian immigrant in Chicago named Israel Warshawsky.

Warshawsky had gone into the mail-order car-parts business in 1934. By 1955, the company was known as J.C. Whitney Co., and there was not a teenage boy alive, whether he owned a car or not, who didn't have the Chicago company's free catalog in his bedroom. That catalog was also on the workbench in the garage at 1310 Bowie.

In 1955, Bill Latimer and his dad, W.W. Latimer, bought a black 1946 Mercury for sixty-five dollars. Of course the car didn't run. In addition to other problems, it had thrown a rod through the pan. But the body and frame were good, and the transmission and rear-end worked. The interior could be made passable with seat covers and black rubber floor mats.

Bill Latimer

They had the Merc towed to the family's garage, and it was at that very moment, 1310 Bowie began its journey toward becoming an important historical place in Galveston, Texas.

In fact, if it were up to me, that garage would now have a cast-aluminum historical plaque on a pole to the left of the driveway, just as Ashton Villa and the Moody Mansion do.

After school, at nights and on weekends, W.W. Latimer channeled teaching his son, Bill, through that 46 Merc—how to grow up, how things work, respect for machines, and the basics of mechanical engineering.

And Bill's dad got to hone and polish his skills at being a good father.

With the help of Warshawsky's J.C. Whitney Co. catalog, they rebuilt the engine with new bored/stroked pistons. They installed a three-quarter racing cam, high compression heads and dual carburetors. They painted the engine block fire engine red. Everything they attached to it was shiny chrome, so that when the hood was open, what you saw was both ominous and beautiful.

They put a dual exhaust system on it with designer mufflers so the car could sound as powerful as it was. Bill Latimer, W.W. Latimer and the garage at 1310 Bowie gained awesome respect among other Island dads and sons.

What had happened in the Latimers' garage, by then, had been taking place in family garages all over America for nearly forty years, as young men worked side by side with their fathers to transform something that had been discarded by another, into a boy's first car.

Today, whether a car runs or doesn't run is governed by a series of computer chips, leaving nothing much that a dad and his son can do together to improve an old car. The once cherished activity of fathers and sons working on cars isn't what it used to be, and most of us from that era mourn its passing.

I wondered what had become of Bill Latimer, and what I found was what I had hoped I would find. An enormous part of his character and interests can easily be traced back to that 46 Merc.

He went to Texas A & M University and got a degree in mechanical engineering. He retired after thirty-two years as an engineer with Monsanto and Sterling Chemicals, and he'd been president of Gulf Coast Water Authority for more than five.

He married another Galvestonian, Don and Ruth Webb's daughter, Vivian. They have two children and three grandchildren. The Latimers have lived in Dickinson for thirty years, where Bill had an elected position on the city council.

What about the cars? He told me his love for cars has never changed. He bought a 56 Ford Thunderbird in 1989, restored it, and won "Best of the Show" with it at the Flowers Annual Show that year. In recent years, he's also owned a Firebird, a Mercedes 560SL, and a Lexus SC400.

What does he now drive? Latimer, just past sixty, apparently decided it was time to appear to the world to be fully grown up. He bought his first four door, a Lexus LS400 sedan. But for the uninformed, let me clarify this for you. Only the outward appearances have changed. That particular car is almost as fast as the 1948 Merc was that he and his dad rebuilt and modified in 1955.

This tale can only leave one to wonder if improved automobile technology and father-son social technology have improved in direct proportion to each other. Sadly, we must consider the overwhelming evidence before us that they have done the opposite.

Joe and Jennings Each Try His Hand at Inventing a Better Lawn Mower

There was a heavenly potpourri odor in the air when Joe Williams was working in the neighborhood. It was one that was never matched by any other circumstance. And not a soul has smelled it since the early 50s.

I have no idea the exact formula, but that sweet smell was comprised of portions of the early morning dew, the blades of St. Augustine grass being individually clipped by a reel lawn mower, and the smoke from Joe's nickel White Owl "ceegar," as they layered themselves on top of the gulf breezes passing the houses of Woodrow Street on their way north.

Joe Williams lived in Hitchcock, but he made the drive to Galveston in his old 38 Ford truck to keep the lawns of special customers. He cut grass with a push reel lawn mower, and, on hands and knees, edged with a hatchet. His finishing touch was weeding and fluffing up the soil in the flower beds with his hoe.

As any summer bored on, pushing a reel lawn mower through the progressively thickening St. Augustine grass would become more and more of a chore.

Nevertheless, every Saturday, Joe would do the lawns of his three customers on Woodrow, all the while puffing on his nickel White Owl ceegar.

During World War II, if a man had a job in a plant making or repairing items needed for America's defense, many times he could be exempted from the draft. Jennings was an MIT graduate. And because he was an engineer for a ship repair company at the dry dock, he was exempt.

He and his wife lived on one of Woodrow's corners and took care of their own lawn.

One time Jennings decided he should use his engineering skills and the machine shop where he worked to make easier his Saturday morning lawn mowing. His idea was to take an old Bendix washing machine motor he had found, build a steel platform on top of his reel lawn mower, weld the Bendix motor to it, and then, through a series of pulleys, sprockets, belts and a bicycle chain, he would invent an electrically powered lawn mower.

Joe wanted to lessen his own lawn mowing burden, too. He didn't have a degree in engineering. In fact, Joe had never gone to school at all, but he had plenty of common sense.

Joe reasoned that what made cutting grass with a reel lawn mower so hard was that when you pushed on the handle to move the mower forward, at the same time, you buried the rear of the mower deeper into the grass. That was what made it hard to push a lawn mower.

As things would have it, one of Joe's customers was

Asa Lee Crow, and Crow owned Gulf Lumber Company. One morning, Joe drove to the lumber yard and asked Crow if there might be a scrap of six-by-six on the floor in the mill that he could have. Lumber was scarce then, and to get even a small board, you had to have connections.

Crow and Joe walked back in the pile of sawdust and found what he needed.

Joe took it home, and over the next several days with his hatchet, a chisel and an old Bowie knife his father had given him years before, shaved the board until it looked like an oversized rolling pin, a rolling pin that was just shy of five inches in diameter.

He replaced the small roller of his reel mower with his newly carved five inch roller. He then drilled new holes in the mower's handle so that it could be lowered, making the grips stomach-high rather than chest-high as they had been before.

If Joe's experiment were to work like he figured it would, the lawn mower's wheels and roller would no longer dig deep into the grass carpet when he pushed. Instead, the lawn mower would ride on top of the grass, so that the energies he expended would primarily be those necessary to cause the reel blades to roll and clip each blade of grass.

Early the following Saturday morning Joe arrived with his modified lawn mower. As you might expect, he drove up in his old 38 Ford truck, while the smoke from his nickel White Owl ceegar was weaving its way out of the windows into the morning air.

As Joe was getting his lawn mower down from the truck bed, Jennings was coming from his garage, pushing his lawn mower down the street. Jenning's mower now had the big Bendix washing machine motor mounted on top, several fan belts in tandem going to a clutch affair, then a bicycle chain going from the sprocket of the clutch to a sprocket he had welded to the blade's axle.

When Jennings got to the front, he pushed the lawn mower up from the street on to the sidewalk, and then he took the long electrical cord he had attached to the motor, and fed the plug-end through the mailbox opening into his living room. There he plugged it in the outlet next to his mother-in-law's glider rocker.

Taped to the lawn mower's handle with many circles of black electrician's tape, was a light switch, just like the ones you have on the walls of your home.

Joe wasn't paying any attention to Jennings. Jennings wasn't paying any attention to Joe. The neighbors, on the other hand, having smelled Joe's nickel ceegar, were looking out of their windows to see what Joe and Jennings were doing.

Now Jennings pulled his motorized lawn mower from the sidewalk onto his yard, faced it toward his house, and then flipped the switch. The thing was so heavy that by then both wheels and the roller had sunk deep into the grass' carpet.

The mower didn't move an inch. Instead it hummed for a second or two, and then rather than move forward to cut the grass, the thing stood still while the motor exploded and smoke and fire shot out of it. Finally it blew a fuse.

Jennings had fallen back to the ground on his rump. The white air raid warden pith helmet he always wore when he was cutting grass had sailed off of his head, and it was now rolling down the street gutter.

That did it. No one could hold back any longer. From every nearby house, belly laughs began coming from the windows. But then sensing that the whole event may have injured Jennings, the neighbors put on their best phoney serious-faces, and ran outside to see if they could help.

Meanwhile, three houses down, and on the other side of the street, Joe Williams' invention was working like a charm. He was all but racing through the grass cutting, as he continued puffing on his White Owl ceegar.

The following Saturday, the neighbors noticed that Joe had added a fourth customer. Fortunately for Jennings, Joe was able to give him membership into his Saturday clientele club, because now Joe had a new, improved reel mower with a hand-carved oversized rear roller and a waist-high handle.

Baby Doll Pajamas, Spoolies and Tabu Marked Rites of Passage

Six of the eight girl friends, who were Lovenberg Jr. High School students, had already accomplished their Rites of Passage. The other two hadn't.

But sometime during that week, the moms of the remaining two girls took them to the Teenage Shop on 45th and Avenue P 1/2 and bought them their first bras. From there they went downtown to E. S. Levy's and got baby doll pajamas and hot-pink fuzzy house slippers. Each got a tube of Charles of the Ritz lipstick. The shade was Be Mine. Then they crossed Postoffice Street to Nathan's and both got a small bottle of Tabu cologne.

Bypassing J.C. Penny's, they went on to Walgreen's. There each got a set of Spoolies and a can of Spray-Net. That completed the uniform. As soon as they could put it all on and modeled for their friends, they could be assured their Rite of Passage to "teenage girl" was a done deal.

With that designation would come an automatic invitation to the weekly slumber party.

The first slumber party that included all eight of the girls was on the following Friday night. It was the night before the Kirwin High School homecoming, and at one of the girl's grandparent's home in Cedar Lawn.

By 8:30 that evening, the old folks were snookered from several too many tumblers of Johnny Walker Red Label and water, and were in their upstairs bedroom in their matching recliners, sound asleep in front of their Hoffman TV.

The eight ruby-lipped girls, dressed in 32-AAs under their baby dolls, hot-pink fuzzy house slippers on their feet, and hair rolled in multi-colored Spoolies, sprayed stiff with Spray-Net, were in the living room listening to Rascal McCaskill's "Night Train" on KREL.

Had anyone then walked through the front door, they would have surely been strangled to death from the overpowering scent of eight bodies, overly sprayed with Tabu cologne.

The girls were drinking RC Colas with a nickel sack of Tom's peanuts dropped in through the bottle necks, eating popcorn, and wishing some boys would call. None did. And there wasn't anything they could do about it. You see, in those days girls didn't call boys.

As kids of both sexes tended to do back then when they were grouped together, out of shear boredom the girls started coming up with dares. Before long, the dares escalated to this one: "I dare all of you to ride the bus with me downtown to the Jean Lafitte Hotel to see my brother. He's the night bellman."

Nobody thought that was much of a dare until they realized that she meant they all had to go dressed like they were. Well, that was asking too much, so the darer amended the petition to, "We'll all put our quilted robes over our baby dolls, but our hair remains rolled up in the Spoolies and the hot pink fuzzy slippers remain on our feet."

After some silly giggling and "My mom and dad would kill me if they found out," comments, it was only a few minutes before the committee of eight was walking to 45th Street and Avenue K to catch the bus to town.

Bus driver George Dillard was on his last run into town. Other than one or two other people on the bus, the girls were the only passengers. Dillard knew them all, and decided to play along with them. He let them off at St. Mary's Cathedral, and they ran giggling across the street to the Jean Lafitte.

Sure enough, as promised, the girl's brother was in the hotel lobby. Bell calls were always slow on Friday nights. And even though he couldn't believe his eyes when the girls first came in, it didn't take him long to recover, and take on the behavior of the older brother.

He told them that the balcony just above the front entrance was just like the one used in performances of Shakespeare's "Romeo and Juliet," and that it would be so funny if they would take the several dozen dead flowers out of the lobby trash can, go out on the balcony, and, pretending to be Juliets, throw flowers one at a time to imaginary Romeos passing by.

Sure enough, the girls fell for the bait, and before long, they were on the balcony with the dead flowers in their hands. But wouldn't you know, just then the Kirwin

Galveston Memories

High School homecoming snake dance came south up 21st Street, then turned and went into the Martini Theater.

"Oh, my God," the girls screamed in unison. They knew the Jean Lafitte was the snake's next destination. Sure enough, back out of the Martini came the snake dance, on its way to the Jean Lafitte.

To get to the lobby, the snake dance would have to go under the balcony. And that balcony had eight ruby red lipped, overly Tabued girls in Spoolies, baby dolls, quilted robes, new but quite frankly useless bras, and fuzzy slippers. And they were holding dead flowers in their hands, looking for imaginary Romeos. What an embarrassment.

Quickly they went to the balcony door to escape their fate. It was locked. Then they heard a crowd cheering, and when they looked down, the snake dance had reformed itself in the middle of Church Street, and it looked much like an unruly Mardi Gras mob demanding beads and doubloons from them.

But it was night and there were no lights on the balcony, so hopefully no one could recognize them, each of the girls reasoned out to herself. Surely the bellman would hear them knocking, he'd open the door, let them in, and save them from an embarrassment that would last a lifetime.

At that moment they became flooded in bright lights from the back of the crowd. That's when they knew that the newest members of their group were having their Rites of Passage filmed, and it would be a part of the KGUL-TV Channel 11 sports news after "Your Hit Parade" on Saturday night.

John W. Cissne: After Thirty Years, Three of the Four Men Saw True Light for the First Time

The three men had been friends throughout their college days. And two of the three had married girls they had met in college. But as things would have it, the men had all but virtually lost track of each other as time had passed, now accruing more than thirty years.

One of their favorite professors, although now retired, still lived in the college town. He had been as much a part of the three men's lives as he would have been had he been the fourth student. Over the years, two of the three had periodically written him, probably for the sense of the security of knowing at least some animate part of their college days still remained among the many old classroom buildings on the small north Texas town's campus.

One decided that all should meet one evening at a restaurant in a city near the campus, to talk about old times, and so that each could recount for the others his life story since they had last been together.

One of the men and his wife picked up the professor at his home, still Ivy League in dress, but this time with a few wrinkles because he was just shy of his seventieth birthday. He was now afraid to drive at night.

The other two, with their wives, were to travel from opposite ends of the nearby big city to the south. All would meet at the restaurant at six sharp. And it happened just as it should have with one exception: One of the men wasn't on time, and he wasn't there by six-thirty either. All began to worry. But as seven on the clock became clearly in sight of a few more minutes, he arrived, his wife a few steps behind him.

He entered the room with the unmistakable smile that they all remembered; the full head of hair with not one gray strand. He wasn't any heavier, and he didn't look any older. However, this time, unlike the last time that they had seen him, he was leading himself with a long white cane, the sure sign of a blind man. All were shocked. Until now no one had known.

After combining hand shakes with bear hugs, they went to their table in the restaurant dining room. Now finished talking about old times—times when they had been together—they then talked about what had happened in each of their lives thereafter.

Tom had been a representative for the U.S. Chamber of Commerce, but after his parents died, inherited just enough money that with wise investing and conservative living, he no longer needed to work. He had married a teacher whom he had met while traveling for the Chamber. Both were actively working to help build the congregation of the Christian Church near their home.

The second man had once done quite well, but had

suffered terrible financial losses and thus found himself faced with starting from the bottom, both in his finances and his self-respect. He was making good progress in the latter, but not much in the former. After a long marriage that had failed, he was ironically now marred to a women they had gone to school with during those very college days.

Ted, the professor, had recently lost his very best friend, one he had known for almost his entire life, but because he was active in one of the local Episcopal parishes, there he had found soul restoration from his grieving.

But it was John, the man with the cane, whose story offered the most. He had been a high-school drama and English teacher, and his wife Susan was a teacher as well. In the evenings he was the stage manager for one of the big city's equity acting companies, a talent he had had and practiced for as long as any of them could remember.

One evening, which coincidentally was the night before one of those plays opened, as John was directing the lighting technician, his sight vanished, just like that. He could see nothing. Fortunately Susan was at his side at the time. She rushed him to the hospital where that night it was determined he had a brain tumor. An operation was needed, and it needed to be done without delay.

John agreed, but he said he was unwilling to be taken into the operating room until the play's opening night had been completed. So from his hospital bed the next evening by telephone and as a blind man, he performed his duties as stage manager, and then said he was ready for the operation to be done the following morning.

Galveston Memories

When the tumor was removed, a good deal of his memory went with it. While he recognized Susan, he knew few others, and he certainly had no retention of anything he had ever learned in sixteen years of school. Hopefully, the doctor said, that would come back later, but there was no hope it would come back at all, without extensive relearning therapy over an extended period of time.

How can an English teacher teach English when he can't spell? That question and others haunted the school district as well as John and Susan. After awhile and after almost thirty years with the district, his teaching contract wasn't renewed.

He was told he would be allowed to substitute teach in the district grammar schools every day. That reduced his income by almost one-half, and the benefits of a contracted teacher were no longer available to him. No medical plan, no teacher retirement, no pay for summer vacation or school holidays, no guarantee that tomorrow he would have work, and no teaching English and drama, the talents that had drawn him to a teaching career in the first place.

But as he told the story that evening, the others holding back their tears, never once did the smile leave his face; never once did he muse for all to hear, "Why did this happen to me?"

Now interestingly, throughout the time the group was together, one of the friends took unposed, arbitrary snapshots to visually and permanently chronicle the evening. When the thirty-six photos were developed, each of the men and women in them had varying facial expressions, as you might have guessed. Some even appeared to have frowns on occasions.

Only one had a smile in every last one of the pictures he was in. As you might guess, it was the one who could now barely see more than the presence of light. It was the man whose necktie this evening had a drawing of a big yellow incandescent light bulb on it.

So what started out to be for the purpose of three old friends and their favorite professor seeing each other again after thirty years took on an entirely different complexion. They now knew that this event was meant to be for the celebration of the life of the sightless man.

One of the bravest and most inspirational men this world has ever known is a person whose name, the chances are, you have never heard, but you'd immediately recognize him if you saw him. He's the blind man with the white cane and the broad smile. His name is John W. Cissne.

Roy Rogers and Sonny Martini: Everyone Mourns the Death of a Good Man

How can it be that Roy Rogers is dead? That he is leaves yet one more void in what is now a rather short list of true super stars, stars that taught American children to go to the movies on Saturday afternoons and that it is only right that the good guy wins.

Back in the late 40s and 50s, there were some seven movie houses in downtown Galveston, each with a single screen. And nearby were specialty stores, department stores, cafes, news and tobacco stands and a handful of barber shops, beer joints pushing Southern Select beer, and bars making out like they weren't pushing Seagram's 7 Crown whiskey. We're talking about twenty square blocks of all of this plus a lot more on the periphery.

This was before the invention of shopping malls, but other than that the downtown wasn't encapsulated in an air conditioned environment, it really had everything a modern shopping mall has.

It was then that Giosue (Sonny) Martini managed for his family the art deco Martini Theater at the corner of 21st and Church Street, and on an Indian Summer Saturday afternoon in 1950, Roy Rogers and Dale Evans were appearing there in "Bells of Coronado."

Galveston Memories

Now for those of you who don't know, since the streets of downtown Galveston were vibrant and full of neighbors, friends and relatives, parents thought nothing of letting their children either ride a city bus by themselves or bicycle to downtown on Saturdays for the special matinee that had a feature film, sometimes two, and always a string of cartoons.

Giosue (Sonny) Martini

On this particular Saturday, in addition to Roy, Dale, Trigger, Buttermilk and Bullet's "Bells of Coronado," the Martini was also throwing in a new movie about gladiators with some Victor Mature look-alike.

We caught the West End bus, driven by George Dillard, and got to town just before Roy, Dale, Pat, Trigger, Buttermilk and Bullet hit the screen. Friends who lived in the nearby East End rode up on their bikes, which had playing cards pinned with wooden clothes pins to the wheel forks so that the cards would slap against the spokes, and thus resemble the sound of a motor bike.

They put the unlocked bikes in the steel tubing rack next to the theater's south wall, and each of us lined up at the box office to pay our nine cents admission to the elderly lady with the big mole on her face, and then joined the others to comprise what would be a full house.

The lights went down simultaneous with the beginning of the clacking of the "Bells of Coronado" film in the projector's sprockets.

You could depend on Roy and Dale to bring a good

story with lots of action and a happy ending. That's what we went for. And the "Bells of Coronado" did just that.

But gladiator shows were even more action packed than Roy Rogers westerns. They had sword fights, shields, and suits of armor, so it was really the gladiator show that sold us on picking the Martini's matinee over the ones running at the other theaters on that particular Saturday.

The second feature started. The gladiators rode in. Immediately the fighting began. A spear was thrown by the Victor Mature look-alike. It was meant to hit one of the enemy horseman. But wait, what is that silver wire running from Victor Lookalike's side to the enemy's chest? I'm not believing this! The spear has hook eyes in it and is traversing down the wire. I swear you can see it! The wire is glistening in the sunlight.

The spear hits its target and the enemy soldier grabs his chest, holds on to the spear, and then falls dead from his horse to the ground. The glistening wire goes with him.

The theater erupts in laughter followed by boos. Victor Lookalike continues on, obviously not noticing himself that his accuracy with the spear was the result of a trick, not his expertise. And he surely is unable to hear the critical unisons of the Martini's audience.

Just about that time, his horse gallops past the castle, and old Victor Lookalike's kneecap accidently brushes against the castle wall. That sets up a ripple in the wall, from bottom to top and back to the bottom again. A stone wall is rippling just like the canvas backdrop does at H.

McKee Andrus' William B. Travis Elementary School's stage! What's going on here?

The laughs and boos erupt again. With that a Siamese cat crosses the bridge over the moat—almost hidden by the horses entering with him, but nevertheless there for the discriminating eye to see is a Siamese cat.

"Look at that cat!" somebody cries. "I see him," says another. "There it is," Ricki Clark yells with delight. More laughs and boos.

With that, Sonny Martini has had enough. The house lights go up, the clicking of the projector sprocket stops, and Victor Lookalike and the gang vanish from the screen as fast as they had come on it at the beginning.

Martini announces that he is ashamed of this terrible movie, and that he is giving everyone their nine cents back, plus a coupon to be used for free admission next week, and furthermore, he is treating everyone to a limeade at the Star Drug Store.

The cheers go up, everybody starts up the two aisles, and sure enough, Martini and his assistant manager refund the admissions, give out the coupons, and tell the kids that Martini has called ahead to Grady Dickinson at the Star Drug Store and everything is all set up for the free limeades.

There is a moral to this story. Everybody is mourning the death of Roy Rogers, just like they did when Sonny Martini passed away some years back. They were both noted to be good and honest men.

Galveston Memories

However, even though I was there and this is my story, not even I can remember the name of Victor Lookalike, nor do I know whether or not he is still alive. Shakespeare wasn't necessarily right. The good that men do does, in fact, often live after them. The bad sometimes doesn't.

Bubba Miller: When Galveston's Big Bopper Was Standing, He Looked Like a Capital S

If you were to see him standing in profile, his form was the shape of a capital S. Tall, somewhat skinny and with a sunken chest, and when he moved there was no question he had all of the flexibility of the double jointed. The head on the S had a big smile and reddish-blond hair combed in a modified ducktail.

His real profession was Ball High School cheerleader, earning the title of Most Popular Boy in his senior year. His avocation, though, was keeping peace in his family by working at his father's service station, Gulf Tire and Supply Co., at the corner of 25th and Broadway, when he wasn't in school. Making grades was way down on his list. It was 1957.

Like many people who, for years, went by a perfectly acceptable nickname, somewhere along the line Bubba Miller decided to become known as Norm Miller, and he's had an interesting life since he left Galveston for the University of North Texas more than forty years ago.

He chronicles that life in an autobiography he wrote with the help of H.K. Hosier, called *Beyond the Norm*, which was published in 1996, by Thomas Nelson Publishers. It contains testimonials of its potential worth to the reader by such notables as Paul Harvey, Tom Landry and Roger Staubach. They're Bubba's friends.

When the name of Bubba Miller enters any of his Galvestonian contemporaries' conversations, the first image mentioned is of him on the dance floor doing his interpretation of the bop, a very interesting and sometimes sexually suggestive dance that was popular with high-school students of the 1950s. Bubba is dressed in a pink longsleeve shirt, charcoal-grey pants held up by a thin pink leather belt, and black and white brogans on his feet that Doug McLeod is sure are as long as Wayne Gaido's—and that's at least a size 12 or 13, maybe bigger.

In that same first breath of the conversation comes the "how did he do that" mention of his luck of being able to convince another Galvestonian, beautiful Anne Kingsbury, to marry him. It seemed so incongruous—Bubba always looking for a party; Anne, quiet, sensible and levelheaded. Perhaps it is the most significant testimonal to Bubba's ability as a salesman.

Nevertheless, somewhere around 1961, they married and moved to Memphis where Anne finished college and Bubba went to work for his father who, by then, had sold his Galveston service station and become a distributor for a new Dallas home based company, Interstate Batteries. Bubba's brother Tommy was working there, too.

Bubba's job was to load up a rent car with batteries and go from service station to service station trying to convince them to sell Interstate batteries. He went all over the country.

He continued his Galveston learned behavior, though, partying, hanging out in bars and, he says, not being a very good husband and father. But that was Bubba, and that's what he thought people, maybe even Anne, liked about him.

The founder of Interstate, John Searcy, became his mentor. As things would have it, Bubba worked hard and progressed up the ladder, by now in Dallas, until Searcy decided Bubba would be his heir apparent. Bubba kept on partying.

In 1974, Bubba decided that irrespective of the enormous gains he had made in the business world, his life was out of control. He had two DWIs, had his license suspended, and here he was drunk and stopped again on Dallas' Central Expressway. But Bubba being Bubba was able to talk his way out of that ticket which would have brought him jail time. He even got the policemen to drive him home.

That's when Bubba decided that it was time for him to truly involve God in his life, and to help God on a plan for him to start that new life. He joined Alcoholics Anonymous, and he and Anne became active in their church.

Fortunately Anne stayed with Bubba through all of his bad years, and was there to join up with him in the new life which became their new life together.

So now Bubba, known to everyone outside of Galveston as Norm, is chairman of Interstate Batteries, the largest name in replacement batteries in the world, selling far more than $10 million a year. His brother, Tommy, is the president.

Bubba and Anne travel to many parts of the world, including Russia, as lay evangalists for such well-known organizations as Campus Crusade for Christ. They are active in the programs of the Dallas Theological Seminary. Bubba and his book have made numerous appearances on such programs as the "700 Club." Shapshots of Anne in the book show her to still be very pretty, defying her age which is now more than fifty.

The University of North Texas was so impressed by all of this, they named Bubba, gray headed and with a full beard, a distinguished alumnus. They had a big reception and dinner for him and the other recipients. That's impressive for a student who worked his way through that very school as its number one bootlegger, a business with sales of sometimes $2,000 a week, all in a dry county that had a fundamentalist church on almost every corner not occupied by a service station.

And while Bubba is now very repentant for the partying behavior he engaged in for thirty years, and perhaps he should be, those who knew him in his days as a bopper are selfishly glad he left Galveston before he found redemption.

Rascal McCaskill: The King is Alive and Living in Victoria, Texas

People in the business called it rhythm and blues. People outside the business more often than not called it race music. Whatever the name, it was the predecessor to rock and roll, and it entered Galveston's and Houston's white teenage markets through a Baytown disc jockey on a tiny heretofore unlistened to AM station at 1360 on the dial known as KREL.

It was 1953, and just home from the service, Bill McCaskill, a white man, got a DJ job at a station in Houston whose call letters were KCOH, and found that the other disc jockeys were not only black but had pseudonyms like King Bee, Dr. Daddy-O, and Hattie Holmes. Not to be different, McCaskill took on the persona of Rascal McCaskill, and replicated the on-the-air patter style of his cohorts.

Let me add that there was one other white person at KCOH in those days, Walter Rubins, the station manager.

As things would have it, the black newspaper voice of Houston at that time, the "Houston Informer," held a contest to pick the top Houston DJ, and KCOH's Rascal McCaskill won hands down. When the paper's photographer was sent to the station to take Rascal's picture for the paper's story, he was astonished to learn Rascal was white. The paper's publisher knew that would never do, so he arbitrarily dropped Rascal to third place, moving up the two black DJs who had really won second and third place.

But understandably that wasn't enough of a compromise, and as a result of the contest and the discovery of Rascal's race, the pressure was on Rubin to replace him with a black DJ, perhaps Daddy Deep Throat.

So in 1954, Rascal moved to all-white KREL, but he brought with him the music he had learned about and played at KCOH, as well as the nickname he had developed for himself.

For the next two years, Rascal's evening program on KREL, "Night Train," single handedly wiped out any significant listener ratings previously held in the Houston market by other music stations, as white teens were fed for the very first time the music of Ruth Brown, Big Joe Turner, Wee Willie Wayne, the Clovers, Ivory Joe Hunter, Johnny Ace and Roy Hamilton.

"Night Train" drew over 100,000 request cards from listeners in 1955. McCaskill's salary went to $150 a week, and he augmented that by fronting sock hops, for after all, with Harris and Galveston county teens, Rascal was as much a celebrity as any of the recording artists he played.

In October, 1954, McCaskill decided rather than playing records at a sock hop, he would experiment with using a live band at one he was putting on in Crosby, just north of Baytown. Because rhythm and blues was so new to the commercial market, there were very few agents booking those groups, and the demand was slim anyway.

Galveston Memories

After much networking, Rascal found an agent in Louisiana who would provide such a band, and the group actually had two recordings on the market. The cost for the three man group for the night was $100. That night they opened with the lead singer's version of "That's All Right (Mama)" and "Blue Moon of Kentucky" followed. Those were the two songs they had recorded.

Two hundred thirty kids heard this group comprised of Bill Black, Scotty Moore and Elvis Presley, for three hours. Six months later the group's new recording, "Heartbreak Hotel," forever changed the whole complexion of the music market.

Bill McCaskill and his wife, Jerry (known to "Night Train" listeners as "Blond Top"), have lived in Victoria, Texas, and have owned and operated the Putt Putt Golf Course for more than twenty-five years. McCaskill is now seventy-two years old. He and Jerry have one son, Billy, a captain in the army, and a grandaughter, Lauren Estelle who was born in October, 1997.

Irrespective of who wishes to take the credit, the King of Rock and Roll in this entire area was Rascal McCaskill, and his reign over "Night Train" (which always ended each evening with its message to its listeners through "You'll Never Walk Alone" by Roy Hamilton from the Broadway musical, "Carousel") is still being recounted by its listeners to this very day.

Bill McCaskill and wife, Jerry

A Lavender 1949 Ford Coupe and a Boy and Girl at the Lagoon were the Root of Envy

Just east of Stewart Beach, and in front of the seawall, is a lagoon that in bygone days was the home of a wonderful private swimming club and restaurant. One of the storms of the late 30s took both out, and they were never replaced. From that point forward the lagoon sat surrounded by a marshland, but with the paved road remaining that connected it to civilization.

In 1956, parked at the water's edge on most nights, was a customized, lavender 1949 Ford coupe. The chrome trim that had surrounded the car when it was new had been removed, and the car had been lowered until it was barely off the ground. Hanging below the rear bumper was a molded cast-aluminum car-club sign. It said Road Runners. From the crowded lover's lane on the Seawall just north of the lagoon, the only light one could see inside the Ford was from the glow of the dial of its AM radio. Like every other radio of a teenager in those days, it was tuned to KREL's Rascal McCaskill's "Night Train."

During the day, the customized Ford was parked at the Ball High campus, for it was owned by a student. But in the evenings it was the only car at the lagoon. That spot, after all, was reserved for it by all of the other lovers, not out of respect for the occupants, but out of respect for the car.

When the Ford was in motion it crept next to the ground, in a sound-aura only dual Mellowtone mufflers could make. Inside was special upholstery that was called "rolled and pleated." It was lavender and white leatherette that was designed, fitted and installed by Fred Fundling's Star Auto Trimmers on 23rd and Church St.

The body modifications and the many coats of lavender lacquer were the work of Henry's Custom Shop, the only thing of note on an otherwise nondescript west end street known as Victory.

The true inspiration for the reality of this car, and the fantasy cars in every other boy's imagination, was a movie, "Rebel Without a Cause," which came to Galveston in 1956. In it, the young star drove a highly polished 1948 maroon Mercury that had been customized.

The lead, played by James Dean, wore jeans and a white tee shirt with a pack of cigarettes rolled in the left sleeve, and a black leather jacket. And he had a haircut whose main feature was ducktails. It required a lot of combing.

Within less than moments of the movie's debut at Galveston's State Theater, high school boys wanted to emulate Dean. The Panama Hotel Barber Shop's Jesse and Joe Mendoza cornered the market on that hair-cut style, just as they had the crew cut only a few years before.

But interestingly, the owner of Henry's Custom

Shop then is today's former mayor Henry Freudenberg. It was in his shop that along with straightening out wrecked cars, standard cars were turned into the customized dreams of their young owners.

And then there was Eddie Hulse's Alamo Auto Parts at the corner of 49th and Broadway that, with the addition of its Mellowtones or Smitty exhaust systems, could make almost any American car at least sound like its next step would be a trip to Freudenberg's for the cosmetic transformation.

As Freudenberg's business prospered, he moved it to 25th and Postoffice where it remained until 1964, when, as things would have it, one of the cars he was working on fell on him, breaking his back. After surgery and months of rehabilitation, it was obvious that the stakes were too high for him to resume his body shop career. The shop was closed.

But coincidentally State Farm Mutual Insurance was beginning to open offices in areas other than rural communities. Hearing about Henry's accident, one of State Farm's home office representatives suggested he apply with the company as the company's first Galveston agent.

From that, his activities in the Galveston Junior Chamber of Commerce and other civic work, as well as his studying to learn the business, Freudenberg became one of the most successful State Farm agents in Texas.

He earned the designation of Chartered Life Underwriter, and ultimately built his office on Stewart Road within a stone's throw of his Victory roots.

Finally, for the purposes of this tale, the owner of the lavender Ford parked at the lagoon and his girlfriend must remain nameless, for each eventually married someone else. But I will tell you this, the boy is an enormously successful life insurance salesman in the Houston area. The girl had fame and recognition as a result of her family, but was glad to see it diminish with adulthood.

Nevertheless, the customized lavender 49 Ford coupe and its part of a moonlighted picture at the lagoon remain a vivid memory to many. No scene before or after was as romantic. Too bad it was never photographed or painted.

George Prader, D.J.

If you know about George and Myrtle Raven's G & M Pleasure Spot on the Mainland, the Down Beat on the sand at West Beach and who George Prader was, you and I are of the same generation, and we are talking about a time when blacks and whites on this island found themselves brought together by a special kind of music.

That particular commonality began the integration of one generation of Galvestonians long before most of the rest of this nation was even beginning to think about desegregation. And it was an interesting set of circumstances that put that into play and caused it to work.

In 1930, George Prader, a black man, was so seriously injured in an automobile accident that he was left almost totally paralyzed. By the late 1940s, another black man, T.D. Armstrong, had made a dynamic success as a businessman here. He had been educated as a teacher, but he moved to Galveston from Louisiana to manage Strode's Funeral Home. Within a short period, he built his own funeral home and from that followed a drug store, a hotel, an insurance company and an accumulation of a great deal of real estate. Later he arranged the financing and was a major stockholder in the 91st Street Fishing Pier along with Howard Robbins and A.R. Schwartz.

Armstrong was also a very active Democrat, to the point that he was one of the authors of the City Charter which changed the Galveston city government into a city manager-council form. He served on the first council under that form, making him the first black man to ever be a council member here.

Now George Prader lived at Armstrong's Little Shamrock Hotel on 37th and Avenue N, and just a couple of years after radio station KGBC went on the air in 1947, with Armstrong acting as the catalyst, James Bradner, Jr., the owner of the radio station, agreed to let Prader become a disc jockey on the station. It was time for Prader to "do something with his life despite his handicap," all three decided, and Prader thought his calling was as a broadcaster.

To make this work, a special remote studio was installed in Prader's bedroom which was on the first floor of the Little Shamrock. A large picture window with a curtain was spread across the front, making Prader's bedroom his proscenium stage so that people driving by, and those going to and from the adjacent drug store, could look in and see Prader when he was on the air. His program traveled down a dedicated telephone line to the KGBC transmitter where The Yacht Club is today, from where it went to the air waves.

Prader lay in his hospital-style bed, a microphone suspended from the ceiling, while his longtime friend, "Red" Mitchell, by day a porter and presser at E.S. Levy & Co., engineered the program each evening, cuing and playing the records as Prader, in his smooth voice, introduced them and talked about the coming entertainment events which would be of the most interest to his black audience.

But it wasn't long until white listeners discovered Prader's "Harlem Express," and they, too, became an integral part of his audience.

Rhythm and blues performers like Ruth Brown, the Clovers, Wee Willie Wayne, Clarence "Gatemouth" Brown, even Roy Hamilton and Ray Charles, were made so popular with Prader's audience, that they were soon making personal appearances at black nightclubs like the G & M Pleasure Spot and the Down Beat, as well as the Pleasure Pier and the City Auditorium.

Interestingly, as a result of Prader's large mixed audience, white listeners who had become both fans of rhythm and blues and of Prader and his "Harlem Express," wondered if they might also be able to buy tickets for those events.

Slowly and under its own momentum, fans of Prader's program started joining together at those places for the personal appearances of the black performers. With Prader's subtle urging, no notice of color was made by the promoters with respect to ticket availability or seating. And it probably didn't occur to those comprising the audience that it should have even been a consideration.

Once, in fact, when a large black review was being staged at the City Auditorium, some city official decided that a rope should be stretched from the back of the house to the stage, dividing the auditorium into two sections, one for whites and one for blacks.

As soon as the curtain went up, the black and white patrons *en masse* took down the rope as evidence of their outrage that anyone would think it proper to segregate the audience. That was never done again.

George Prader and the twelve-year run of his "Harlem Express" did more on this island to teach the silliness of segregation than any other person before or after him. From that he gained national recognition when articles appeared about him such publications as "Jet Magazine."

George Prader died December 30, 1961. His studio on 37th and Avenue N, by the curtain remaining closed for years thereafter, was a visual memorial to him.

"Red" Mitchell, now retired, lives to tell the stories of that remarkable man whom I am proud to say was my friend.

George Prader, D.J.

Love

At Miss Dorothy's: Arthur and Summer Saw the Midnight Sun

Her name was Summer, and she was exactly the person you are envisioning right now. Straight and perfect teeth behind full lips shaded with deep-red Charles of the Ritz lipstick. High cheek bones just below green eyes. Full, shoulder-length chestnut hair, always shining, even when only in the light of a quarter moon.

Summer was just nineteen at the time, and it was for sure no one thought she looked older, or younger, for that matter. I'd say she was about five and a half feet tall, maybe one hundred twenty pounds. But it was her twenty-two inch waist that made her figure appear to be the one every girl her age wished she had. And Summer had a lovely walk in high heels, while most girls her age wobbled in them.

Summer was from Dallas, and she was a sophomore physical education major at Sam Houston State Teachers College in Huntsville. She wanted to be a high school tennis coach.

Her dad was a free-lance news photographer, but he sold most of his work to Life Magazine, making Summer wonder why he just didn't work for Life full-time. Her mother spent most of her time shopping at Highland Village stores. Summer had one brother. He was eleven. As a family, most Sundays they went to the Methodist church over by SMU.

Now in those days, the Galveston boys called them "cat houses." When the newspaper reported on the latest raid, they referred to them as "bawdy houses." In their Sunday sermons, preachers preferred to call them "houses of ill-repute." Others who thought those terms hauteur called them something more down to earth.

And in the 1950s, contrary to what you may have been told, the true well-decorated, well-staffed Galveston cat houses were mainly on Market Street, not west Postoffice Street. They didn't have rinky-tink pianos with piano players, and there were no fights, ever. Dorothy Malone, Jesse Dixon and Margaret Lera were the cat houses' well-known proprietors.

And furthermore, you can forget what you've seen in the movies. The Galveston cat houses were noted for their young, well-mannered, beautiful girls. And those young and beautiful girls had exceptional manners and were dressed in the finest of clothes from Nathan's, E.S. Levy's and Leopold's. Miss Jesse, Miss Dorothy and Miss Margaret would have it no other way. And no one worked there to support a drug habit because they didn't have drug habits.

Other than a juke box that was in the living room of each cat house, they were decorated, furnished and otherwise appointed as nicely as any fine Island home. The juke boxes had records of carefully selected dance music and beautiful jazz. Cocktails were sold and served, and it wasn't bootlegged whiskey either. It was the best. And the bars were hidden away in rooms the clientele never saw. I know it's an oxymoron, but the cat houses here were genteel.

Now it was the day after Thanksgiving in, I think, 1957, and as high school and college boys around here frequently did after their dates, Buddy and Arthur, home from Sam Houston State Teachers College, decided to stop in at Miss Dorothy's to dance and visit with a couple of the girls in the living room.

Up the stairs above the liquor store they went. Arthur was taller and looked older, so he rang the doorbell. Miss Dorothy slid back the peephole door, recognized Arthur, and let the two boys in.

It was then that they saw a girl dressed in a strapless, deep maroon evening gown. They looked at each other frozen-faced, because the person they saw looked like Summer, the co-ed at Sam Houston State that each of them had secretly wanted to ask out, but had been afraid to. They had thought surely she would turn them down.

Buddy said to Arthur in an almost inaudible whisper, "That's not Summer!" As Arthur was taking a breath to respond, he inhaled the familiar scent of Joy perfume. His fear was confirmed. Summer always wore Joy. Her mother got it at Neiman's for Summer and her.

Arthur split from the twosome, and went over to Summer, offered his hand, and she came close to him, and they began to dance. From the juke box the mellow roar of the baritone sax in the Stan Kenton Orchestra decended the scale and then June Christie sang, "Your lips were like a red and ruby chalice, warmer than a summer night. The clouds were like an alabaster palace, rising to a snowy height. . . ."

Someone, probably the bouncer, had left a bamboo stool against the north wall, near the door. The whole circumstance was making Buddy's head spin. He felt dizzy and was sure he was going to barf. He climbed up on the stool and watched as Arthur and Summer, bodies so close, danced to the beat of "Midnight Sun." Neither Arthur nor Summer spoke a word.

And the song ended, ". . . but oh my darling I'll always remember when your lips were close to mine, and I saw the midnight sun; see the midnight sun above?"

Summer went to her tip-toes as she kissed her index finger, and placed the kiss on Arthur's forehead. Until then he had never noticed how small and delicate her hands were. Still not one word was exchanged between the two.

Arthur turned and walked across the room to Buddy. Miss Dorothy opened the door for them, and they went down the twenty or so steps to the sidewalk on Market Street. A society party at the beachfront Marine Ballroom had just ended, so Market Street was packed with the guests on their way to Jesse Lopez's Rio Grande Club for breakfast. It was about 1:30 on Saturday morning. Buddy and Arthur said nothing as they weaved their way through the crowd.

When the two boys got to Arthur's deep-black lacquered 56 Chevy Impala, Buddy said, "It was Summer, wasn't it?" "Yes, it was Summer." A pact was made at that very moment. Neither would ever tell anyone what they had seen. And they would never, ever discuss it again. They kept that pact for just shy of forty years. In fact Arthur only told me about it this past November.

It was in 1964, that Arthur was standing in the Braniff Airways ticket line at the Dallas airport. By then he was an accountant for a large firm, and he was on his way to Chicago to lead an audit for one of its clients.

Oddly, a flashback came to mind. It was 1957, again, and in his mind's eye he saw Summer—her soft smile, green eyes and the figure punctuated by the twenty-two inch waistline. For that brief moment they were again in the surroundings of the campus at Sam Houston State Teachers College. She had on her tennis shorts and a starched white blouse. She was not in the maroon evening gown dancing with him in Miss Dorothy's cat house. He loved the Summer he was seeing now.

It was then that his flashback was interrupted by the realization that he was smelling Joy, the perfume marketed by the manufacturer as "the most expensive perfume in the world." Summer was the only person he had ever known who wore it. Then he knew that's what had, only a moment before, brought into his mind's eye the vignette from their past life as Sam Houston State students. Summer must be nearby, he thought.

A smile came on his face, honest it did, and he turned toward the airport lobby to see if Summer would be there for him once again. And she was.

As he walked toward her she was smiling, and he began singing to her, "Your lips were like a red and ruby chalice, warmer than a summer night. The clouds were like an alabaster palace, rising to a snowy height. I can't explain the silver rain that found me, or was that a moonlit day...." When he reached her, Arthur put a kiss on his index finger and placed it on her forehead.

But without the exchange of a single word, Arthur turned away from Summer, and with his ticket in hand, left for the runway where the plane to Chicago was boarding.

The Story of Ski, and Antoinette and Jesse Belvin, the Rhythm & Blues Singer

Of all of the people I know who knew him, like I, not one could tell you what his wife's name was. In fact, I don't know that any of us ever met her.

But everyone knew Ski. When he wasn't at work at his government job, he was bowling. He was a member of at least two leagues at every bowling alley in the city. Someone told me he consistently maintained an average well above 180.

While after work Ski's passion was bowling, his wife's was watching television and eating M&Ms.

Antoinette was recently divorced. She was thirty-two years old and had one daughter who was ten. Antoinette worked as a hostess at a restaurant during the day, and at the counter at one of the bowling alleys at night. She needed every dime she could get her hands on to support herself and her daughter. She couldn't depend on her ex-husband regularly sending the $35 a month child support. That he was unreliable was the reason they had divorced.

Antoinette always wore a starched white cotton blouse, black slacks with stirrups, white socks and red sneakers. She had short black hair, and a pretty olive complexion with pores so small you had to get close to see them. The only jewelry she wore was a replica of Arlene Francis' diamond heart-shaped necklace, gold ear studs, and the clunky silver ID bracelet her ex-husband had given her after he had come home from Korea.

Since Ski and Antoinette were both at the bowling alley every night, it wasn't long before they began drinking coffee together and chatting while he was waiting for the next league to start. One night her neighbor was unable to baby sit, so Antoinette brought her daughter to the bowling alley. That's when Ski met her. Ski and his wife had no children, and Antoinette's daughter, for all practical purposes, had no father. At that first meeting, it took less than ten minutes for Antoinette's daughter and Ski to bond.

The friendship of Ski with Antoinette and her daughter continued to grow at a profound rate. One Saturday night, after the last league had finished and the bowling alley had closed, Ski invited Antoinette to go with him and his team for a victory after-party at the old Gizmo Bar. It was Thanksgiving time in 1956.

The Gizmo's jukebox selections were mainly the latest country-western tunes, a smattering of World War II big-band songs, and the one by Bing Crosby that no one ever played, "Swinging on a Star." Oddly, now there was an incongruous addition, a popular new rhythm and blues ballad, "Good Night My Love" by Jesse Belvin. Ruby, the barmaid, had had it put on the juke box.

Ski and Antoinette rode together to the Gizmo in Ski's 1954 black Ford coupe. As they walked in, the jukebox was cranking up Belvin's song.

"Good night my love. Pleasant dreams and sleep tight, my love. . . ."

Ski said to Antoinette, "If we're ever going to dance together, we'd better do it now. It's probably the only slow one Ruby has on that thing, and it's probably the only time we'll ever be anywhere together other than the bowling alley."

Belvin continued, "May tomorrow be sunny and bright, and bring you closer to me. Before you go, there's just one thing I want to know. . . ."

The others from the league started to arrive, as the song was ending. Everyone grinned as Ski and Antoinette finished with a dip, a dance move that was so outdated by then that even Ski and Antoinette could no longer do it gracefully.

After that night, it didn't take long for Ski and Antoinette to become a couple, at least a couple in the eyes of those who spent their time at the bowling alleys. And no one seemed to think there was anything wrong with that relationship since Ski's wife, for all practical purposes, didn't exist in their eyes.

Ski started to help Antoinette when she was short of money. He insisted that her daughter enroll in Catholic school, so he paid for her tuition and uniforms.

By the time two years or so were up, the only thing

that kept Ski, Antoinette and her daughter from looking like a family was that Ski didn't sleep at their apartment at night.

Just before Antoinette's thirty-sixth birthday, she went to get a checkup for a health card. Health cards were required in those days to handle food. Occasionally, Antoinette would work in the bowling alley concession. She went to her family doctor for the checkup. He found a suspicious lump in her left breast.

Quickly Antoinette checked into St. Mary's Infirmary. The breast was removed and shortly thereafter, she learned that the cancer had metastasized, The oncologist told her that even with aggressive treatment her chances of living past Christmas were slim.

Antoinette had no close family. Her mother and father had been dead for at least ten years. Her one sister lived up north. Antoinette's main concern was who would take care of her daughter after she was no longer able to. Her ex-husband, she thought, would be a terrible choice. It should be Ski.

It was then that the truth, the real truth could no longer be ignored. Ski had no plans to leave his wife. In fact, he was never going to admit to his wife his love affair with Antoinette. He was certain that she would never suspect it on her own.

The sicker Antoinette got, the less frequently Ski came by to see her and her daughter. When school started the following September, he made some excuse about no longer being able to pay the little girl's tuition and uniform expense. She'd have to go to public school.

Just before Easter the following year, Antoinette passed away. She had not seen Ski in two months. He hadn't called, or sent flowers, not even a card.

Her sister came to make the funeral arrangements. She called Ski to see if he would sit with Antoinette's daughter in the family pew at Malloy's Funeral Home. Ski said he couldn't do that. How would he explain that to his wife if she were to find out?

Antoinette's sister then asked Ski if he would be a pallbearer. No, he said.

On the morning of Antoinette's funeral, it was a cool Galveston spring day. Ski parked his 54 Ford coupe across Broadway from Malloy's and he slumped down in the seat so no one could see him. From there he thought he'd watch.

Malloy's funeral director, Tommy Leatherberry, looked out of the funeral home office window. He and Ski had been friends for years. He knew a great deal about Ski's and Antoinette's relationship, a relationship he had never approved of. He knew it was Ski in that car that was across the street.

Right then Leatherberry picked up the office phone and called Mel Pennington, the morning disc jockey at KGBC. Leatherberry and Pennington knew that whenever their friend Ski was in his Ford, his car radio was tuned to KGBC. They came up with a plan.

At 10:35, Leatherberry, driving the family car, began leading Antoinette's possession out of the funeral home driveway. At that very moment, Pennington announced over the air that an old friend of his had asked that he dedicate a song to her friend, Ski. "It was their song," Pennington said.

With that, Jesse Belvin began to sing, "Good night my love. Pleasant dreams and sleep tight my love. May tomorrow be sunny and bright, and bring you closer to me. Before you go, there's just one thing I'd like to know. Is your love still warm for me, or has it grown cold . . ."

Now crying, Ski could stand it no longer. He started up his car, quickly U-turned, and raced to break in line behind the hearse carrying Antoinette to the cemetery.

More than half of the car radios of those in the procession were also tuned to KGBC. One by one they rolled down their windows and turned up their radios, so that the world could hear Belvin as he continued to sing one last time for Antoinette and Ski.

"If you should awake, in the still of night, please have no fear. For I'll be there. You know I care. Please give your love to me, dear only. Good night my love. Pleasant dreams, and sleep tight my love. May tomorrow be sunny and bright, and bring you closer to me."

Smooching Can Make a Boy and Girl Say Things They Don't Mean

He swears this is exactly how it happened.

The two of them had grown up less than a city block apart. They had never been more than friends. But wouldn't you know that just before she was to go away for six weeks to a girls' summer camp, Camp Mystic in Hunt, Texas, they tried open-mouth smooching behind her garage a couple of times for the heck of it, and their new-found hormones sent them a revelation: They were now in love.

They had finished the seventh grade, and as soon as this summer would end, they would be in the eighth.

That following Saturday morning, even before the sun had thought about coming up, her entire family set out in the family car for Camp Mystic, where Leigh would practice swimming and diving, make some lanyard key chains out of flat plastic rope, cover a few wire coat hangers with the same flat plastic rope, turn over in a canoe a handful of times, learn archery, destroy nearly a thousand dollars of her parents' money in the process, and over and over tell everyone there how much she missed her new boyfriend.

Before she had left, however, Leigh and her boyfriend had made a pact, almost in blood. They would write each other every day, even on Sundays. Both of them did keep their promises.

Part of writing a love letter in those days was to not hide from the postman or anyone who might later see it on the recipient's dresser, what kind of letter it was. The writer would print a code in several places on the outside of the envelope: SWAK. It wasn't a secret code. Everyone knew it meant "sealed with a kiss." Drawn around the SWAKs, were hearts with arrows shooting through them.

Every SWAK letter was saved, filed in chronological order, and reread from beginning to end, time and time again, from the first letter to last. Someday after they had been married for many years, maybe on their fiftieth anniversary, they figured they would pull them out and reread them. After all, those letters would chronicle the beginning weeks of their love affair.

Finally the six weeks were up, and the day came for Leigh to come home from Camp Mystic. It was a Sunday, and she was to arrive about noon. Both Leigh and her boyfriend had wondered if this day would ever come.

His parents thought it would be a swell gesture if they were to go to the Chow Line at the corner of 23rd Street and Avenue O and pick up a sack full of hamburgers and French fries from the guy who worked there. He had been affectionately given the nickname of Creeping Jesus by the Kirwin High School boys. And everyone called him that, even the boy's parents.

While the boy's mom and dad were on their way to see Creeping, the phone at home rang. It was Leigh. She was coming over early. She couldn't wait any longer to see him.

He went out to greet her, and sure enough, there she was walking down the sidewalk toward him. She had on white short-shorts, one of those crinkly red halter tops, white sandals, and her hair was in a kazillion pin curls all partially covered by a red nylon scarf. Her tan legs looked wonderful. Moments before she had made her lips especially smoochable with a too heavy application of the extremely popular Revlon lipstick shade, "It's Plum Red!"

When she was less than a half block away, she raised her arm to wave. He could see the white stain under her arm that was there from the two poofs of Stopette deodorant she always wore. She once had told him that if Stopette were good enough for the glamorous Arlene Francis and Dorothy Kilgallen on "What's My Line?", it was good enough for her.

But it was at that very moment that they made the same instantaneous decision. They were not in love, and they really didn't particularly want to see each other. They didn't even want to smooch one last time before they parted ways.

When they finally were face to face, she heard herself saying, "I'm not in love with you," and they both heard an unmistakable sigh of relief coming from him. She turned and retraced her path home, and he went to his bedroom and got the bundle of her love letters out of the cigar box that he kept on his clothes closet shelf.

The letters must be destroyed, he thought. This would be the only way he would be able to exorcise this whole chapter from his life. Tearing them up and putting them in the trash can wouldn't do. They must be burned to ashes.

So, he took them out to the alley behind his house, put them in a pile on the street, and then dowsed them with gasoline from the can that was used to fill his dad's power lawn mower.

With that, he stood over the gasoline-drenched pile, struck a wooden kitchen match on his right shoe sole, and then threw the match into the middle of the pile of SWAK letters.

BANG! The gas can was now flying across the street with a trail of flames following behind it. Within a second or two, it slammed into a wall of the garage apartment two doors to the west, went through it and disappeared into its living room.

Now his ears were ringing beyond belief. The hair on his arms was gone. And he didn't have eyelashes or eyebrows anymore. And the front of his crew cut was singed, and he smelled like burned hair and melted Butch Wax.

If that wasn't bad enough, he heard the Ford coming down the driveway. It was his mom and dad with the sack full of hamburgers and fries from Creeping Jesus at the Chow Line. What was he going to tell them?

The minute they got out of the car, they not only smelled the singed hair and melted Butch Wax, but they also saw their son was now without eyebrows and eye lashes.

As hard as he tried, in his mind their son was unable to come up with a logical excuse, so he just decided he'd better confess and pay the consequences that were sure to come.

He did figure, though, that his parents didn't need to know the part about the gasoline can sailing across the alley and disappearing into the living room of the garage apartment, so he left that out.

His dad was wise, and as he listened to the story, he wondered what had happened to the gasoline can. It was then that he saw the hole in the wall of the garage apartment.

The hamburgers would have to wait. Now the boy must go over to the neighbor's house, ring the doorbell, tell the man what had happened, apologize, and offer to pay for the damages.

So I asked my friend, "What was the lesson you learned from all of this?" figuring he would say something like the dangers involved when striking a match around gasoline. But that wasn't it.

Instead he said, "Never destroy a letter from a friend, no matter what. Save every one of them." And that's exactly what he has done for the past forty years. And he keeps them in chronological order, too.

Everyone Needs to Go Into His Cave From Time To Time

Modern day counselors refer to it as "going into your cave." A "cave" is that special place each of us goes to be alone when we need to make peace with ourselves.

She had found that her cave was a certain rock groin pier that extended from the seawall. Anytime she needed to resolve a major problem, she'd get her fishing gear, stop at Negrini's for a mess of cut bait, and head for that groin where she would fish for hours.

On this particular day, it was unusually cold. A light rain was falling. The chance of catching fish was next to nil. The chance of catching pneumonia was better than good. But she knew she had to go to her cave. She couldn't wait for a better day.

Bundled up in warm rain gear from head to toe, and after she had been fishing alone on that groin for a couple of hours, she noticed about halfway between her and the seawall, another fisherman had come equally bundled up.

It wasn't long thereafter that her hook got caught between rocks at water's edge. No matter how she maneuvered her line, it wouldn't come free. She looked up, and the other fisherman was standing next to her.

"You hold your rod and keep the line tight, and I'll work my way down on the rocks and see if I can free it," he suggested. And within minutes, the hook was loose.

Thankful, she introduced herself to him, and he, in turn, introduced himself to her, at which time they both laughed. You see, years before while students at Lovenberg Jr. High, they were in love, but her father had forbidden them to date because he felt they were too young.

They were sure they had found in each other their intended lifelong mate, and that her dad was interfering with God's will, but no amount of reasoning would change her father's mind.

So after the reintroductions on this cold, rainy day, they walked over to a beachfront coffee shop to catch up on the past forty years. She learned that he had just divorced, and had gone to the groin to decide his future, for it was his cave as well.

Both admitted that her father's position had, in fact, haunted them for years, because surely their hearts had been correct, and had he let them date, eventually they would have married, have had their family, and would be living happily together to that very day.

Instead, both had suffered through marriages to others that had bitterly ended in divorce.

So he and she decided that their chance meeting on

such a day on a rock groin in Galveston after forty years was fate, and that they should resume where they left off in junior high.

This time it would play out for them as it should have before, they agreed.

For the next few weeks they were a couple. But then it came time for them to recognize that romance for them was never meant to be. Her father had been right after all but for the wrong reason.

They parted friends, but at least with one question answered that had haunted each of them for forty years.

Caves are such good places to solve problems.

The First Girlfriend, The First Date

Trying to work up the courage to ask a girl out when you're thirteen, and if she says, Yes, it will be your first date ever, was just as frightening in 1954, as it probably is to any thirteen-year-old boy in 1999.

Add to it that the event would be the annual Lovenberg Jr. High sock hop, and the girl you thought you loved was at least four inches taller than you. I know you know that would take a double-dose of courage. Forget the part about not knowing how to do anything other than the box step.

And there was no way this was going to be a grown-up experience. After all, if you got past all of that in the first two paragraphs, your mom was still going to have to drive you to and from the dance in the family's black 1952 Ford four-door. Gad, what a nightmare!

Nevertheless, somehow I was able to pull this off in the spring of 1954. My date had a complexion that looked as if she had a year around suntan, and not a zit one. And she had shoulder length brown hair and brown eyes. I thought she was beautiful, and as I look back now, I know she was.

The sock hops were held in the school gym. They were called sock hops because leather sole shoes weren't allowed near the gym's waxed varnished floor. And we didn't wear Reeboks and Adidas in those days because they hadn't been invented, so to dance on the gym floor, we had to do it in our socks, hence "sock hop."

Not much happened at this sock hop. The attendees all tried to look like they weren't embarrassed, hardly anyone danced, and for the most part, the boys ended up on one side of the gym, the girls on the other. All the while, Jo Stafford's "Make Love to Me" echoed over the P.A. system a zillion times in a row. Now and then whoever was in charge substituted one round of the Mills Brothers' "Glow-Worm," but for the most part, it was a one-song sock hop.

And except for when everyone lined up to do the bunny hop, in most cases the next time the boys got together with their dates was when it was time to go home.

I'm proud to be able to say that my date and I awkwardly box stepped through one of those repeats of the Jo Stafford song. And the lyrics, "Put your arms around me, darling, hold me tight. Whisper to me gently while the moon is bright," were so ridiculous. I thought, "None of that is going to happen for me."

However, from then on, and for the next couple of years thereafter, she and I were a team. We did everything together. Thank goodness she was a tomboy. And then somewhere along the way we shifted to being pals. She got a steady boyfriend, and I went through a handful of girlfriends.

And then she went off to boarding school, so I only saw her on those occasions when she was home for the holidays. As friends, we'd write, and sometimes my parents would let me call her long distance. Throughout it all, oftentimes I wished we were still a team.

Finally she went away to college, got married, moved to California and had two daughters. I didn't see her or hear from her for nearly forty years.

But then by sheer happenstance, about four years ago I got out of my car and walked toward Eckerd Drugstore. As I approached the store, I passed a lady who was coming out. Minutes later, the same lady who had been leaving was standing next to me in the store aisle, and she was saying, "Aren't you Bill Cherry?"

It was she, my first date, and since the height difference between us hadn't resolved over time, she was again unconsciously rounding her shoulders and stooping. We hugged and kissed and found ourselves continuing to hold hands as we chatted. I was so glad to see her.

But our visit lasted for just minutes, I'd say less than five, because it was hot outside, and her nearly ninety year old mother was waiting for her in the car. We vowed that we would somehow get together soon. After all, in those days I made frequent trips to Los Angeles, and she lived in nearby Beverly Glen.

As she was leaving down the drugstore aisle, I

called out an afterthought, "I still have the picture you gave me in 1957; the one of you that was in the St. Stephen's School yearbook. It's framed and on my piano." I knew from her smile that she was pleased.

Sandy Williams, 1957

I never got so see her again. Our lifelong friend, Doug McLeod, called on March 3, to let me know that my first girlfriend, Sandy Williams Graham, had died after a nine-month fight with inoperable brain cancer. The residents of heaven have gotten someone special. I have our memories and the picture of her as a seventeen-year old. Like I said, it's framed and on my piano.

Rose, Curly, the Priest and the Doctor above the Dime Store

Although English teacher Helen Robinson had formed the True Readers to be a girls' reading club, even back then Ball High School students called it the TR's, and to them it was a school sorority.

One Saturday night, six of the TR's set out for the Tokio, which was a two-story, open-air building where the Beach Central is today. There was dancing on one floor, a roller rink on the other.

This was the day after the public schools had had their traditional May Fetes, and that signaled that soon the school year would end, to be followed by three months of vacation. This year would be no different, even though there was a war going on in Europe.

The six TR's hadn't been at the Tokio for more than ten minutes, when one of them, whom I'm going to call Rose, made eye contact with a soldier. As the band was doing its best to mimic the Glenn Miller Orchestra, he came across the floor, introduced himself as Curly, and asked her for a dance.

Even though, by then, they had known each other for less than two minutes, they were dancing far closer than just acquaintances.

For the remainder of the night, they sat at a table for two at the southeast corner of the dance floor. When they danced, it was confined to a tiny spot of vacant floor next to their table.

It came time to leave. Rose and Curly were nowhere to be found. His army buddies went back to Fort Crockett without him. Her friends went on to the slumber party.

Rose and Curly saw each other three more times, the last time was when she went with him to a movie at the Fort Crockett base. He said he would write. He didn't.

By mid-August Rose's fears were confirmed by the old doctor. He was a pediatrician, but the only doctor she had ever used. Curly hadn't written, she would soon begin her senior year at Ball High, and the doctor had told her she would be having a baby near St. Valentine's Day.

Rose's father was Catholic, her mom, agnostic. They were professional people. Rose had gone to St. Mary's Cathedral elementary school, but because of the differing religious beliefs of her parents, she was unclear as to her own. The only godly things she knew for certain were that she loved both Father Dan O'Connell at St. Mary's Cathedral, and the gold crucifix necklace that neighbors had given her when she made her first communion.

When she reached junior high school age, she asked

her parents if she could leave Catholic school and go to Stephen F. Austin Jr. High. They agreed. Rose never went to Mass again, and her gold crucifix stayed in her jewelry box.

Now she was faced with her first adult decision, a decision that not one of her friends or even a distant acquaintance had faced before her, at least not that she knew of.

She had heard about women going to Mexico where abortions were performed in unsanitary conditions, and where many bled to death from faulty procedures.

Rose asked the old doctor to break the law and terminate her pregnancy before anyone else found out. He told her that he wouldn't, but he would tell her of a physician in Houston, whose office was on an upper floor of one of the dime store buildings, who might help her. The old doctor turned around to his typewriter, and typed the doctor's name and address on a scrap of paper. He gave it to Rose.

The next morning, without making any attempt to get an appointment, Rose dressed in her navy blue pleated skirt and a blue cotton sweater over a Peter Pan collar. She planned to add her pearl necklace, but when she took it out of her jewelry box, it was kinked. She put the gold crucifix on instead, something she hadn't done in at least four years.

She walked to the bus station a few blocks away, and with the withdrawal from the savings account her grandmother had established for her college fund, she had in her purse the $250 medical fee and bus fare.

The entrance to the upper-floor offices was to the west of the dime store. The lobby looked seedy, but she had to take the chance. After all, the old doctor had told her she would be safe. She took the steps rather than the elevator.

The waiting room was small, the chairs were oak straight-backs. There was one other woman there. The nurse called in Rose.

The doctor and Rose sat down across from each other at the doctor's desk. He asked her the same questions that the old Galveston doctor had asked, but this doctor told her that he was going to put her name in his records as Mary St. John. She wondered why he made up that particular name.

He asked her if she was from Houston. She said, no she was from Galveston. It was obvious that he had noticed her gold crucifix necklace. Why else would his next question have been, "Do you know Father Dan O'Connell?"

She didn't want to answer, but since she flinched and looked down at her lap, the doctor had his answer. He went on without waiting for her response. He told her that he, himself, was a Lutheran, and that his son was in medical school in Galveston. His last year. It was also the doctor's alma mater.

He said that as an intern, one Friday he was sitting at the lunch counter at the Central Drug Store on Postoffice Street when Father Dan came in for an egg salad sandwich. The priest took the stool next to him. From that chance meeting, a friendship developed.

The doctor told Rose that about ten years later, he got a phone call from Father Dan. The priest said that he had heard that the doctor was performing a procedure which was against God's law and criminal law as well.

The doctor said he told Father Dan that he felt he was doing what God wanted him to do: save desperate women from the butchers of Mexico. Father Dan was unable to build a case convincing enough for the doctor to agree to stop.

The doctor told Rose that he did promise Father Dan that he would never perform the procedure on any woman he knew or suspected to be a Catholic.

"You know Father Dan, don't you," the doctor again asked Rose. "Yes, sir," she said. With that the doctor picked up the receiver of the telephone, dialed the operator, and asked to be connected to the rectory at St. Mary's in Galveston.

"Father Dan?" Before he had a chance to add his name, the priest recognized his friend's voice and said, "Yes," then called him by name.

"I'm sending Mary St. John to see you. You will know her by another name, her real name. She needs the Catholic God's help and your guidance."

Rose caught the next bus to Galveston, and Father Dan was waiting for her when she stepped off. He did remember her, and when he saw the gold crucifix around her neck, he remembered it, too.

In 1947, Rose was sitting with her two-year-old

daughter on her parents' porch. It was afternoon, but the sun was now being hidden by the home next door. Rose was starting to get cold. Her baby must be, too. Just as she stood up and prepared to take her daughter inside, she was shocked to see a familiar face at the front gate. It was Curly. It had been three years.

It wasn't long thereafter that Rose and Curly were married. Father Dan performed the ceremony. It was done on a Wednesday after the regular noon Mass. Her mother, father and sister plus an altar boy were the only invited witnesses.

The other witnesses were those who had remained after the Mass to pray their special petitions. One of them was kneeling near the back of the church. He smiled at Rose and Curly as they walked down the aisle for the first time as man and wife. He was a Lutheran physician from Houston.

Ardella Connor and the Rubaiyat of Omar Khayyam

When Ardella Connor came to Galveston, she was a single mom of Swedish-German extraction from Minnesota who had been a martial-arts instructor in the women's branch of the Marine Corps. She was still in her twenties.

From the beginning, the financial life of Ardella and her young daughter, Vicki, was, at best, touch and go. Many days there was only enough money to buy soup and coffee, and that was with Ardella working two eight-hour jobs as a waitress.

But fate stepped in, and Ardella found her way to a corner on 23rd Street, near the beach. It was a lucky corner and it had been, by then, for more than forty years.

It had been the place where Mike Mitchell, Galveston's most famous Greek immigrant, had gotten his start in business with a cleaning and pressing shop. It was where his sons, Johnny and George, as children, learned their work ethics, later to become multimillionaire oilmen.

And it was in the Snug Harbor café, that was next door

to the cleaning and pressing shop, where Louise Bird had met the financial backer that had helped her to become the founder and owner of Galveston's most famous nightclub ever, the Pirate Club.

Christie Mitchell, Galveston's legendary publicist, also a son of Mike Mitchell, had rented the upstairs of the Snug Harbor building from his dad, made it a nightclub and named it the Omar Khayyam.

Meanwhile, Ardella was saving and wisely investing her money. In the summers and in her bikini, she saved many pale-skinned tourists from sunburn as she walked the beach applying Tartan Suntan Lotion for fifty cents an application. "Have Tartan, Will Apply," the sign on her shoulder bag proclaimed.

Tartan paid her a hundred bucks a month and supplied their products to her at no charge. The hundred bucks, the fifty cent fees and the tips mounted up fast.

In the evenings, she was one of the "garter girls" at caricaturist Claude Allen's famous Golden Garter Club on the beachfront Pleasure Pier. The garter girls were part of the melodrama show and were waitresses.

When Christie Mitchell decided to sell his Omar Khayyam club, and Mike Mitchell decided to sell the building, Ardella bought both and paid cash. And that was when the Omar Khayyam really had its awakening.

Ardella sewed drapes for the interior and made Arabian costumes for herself, her waitresses and her bartenders. The outfits were scant, flimsy and semitransparent, and all that wore them had a semiprecious stone affixed to their navels.

The club was dark and looked like our imaginations said a sultan's tent should look. There were paintings and statuary from Turkey, India, the Far East and Ethiopia. There were figurines from Indonesia. And most of those were the real McCoys, having been brought to Ardella by bankers, oil men, sea captains and importers whose businesses had taken them to those exotic places.

There was King Tut, Buddha and Queen Nefertiti and a wonderful portrait of Ardella in her costume that had been done in the pastel medium by Eleanor Sullivan.

Ardella made more than forty of the Arabian costumes and made them in popular women's sizes. Men brought their wives and girlfriends to the Omar Khayyam, and while they were Ardella's guests, they could dress up in one of the many costumes and have their picture taken in the "sultan's tent."

Somewhere along the way, Ardella met an Italian seaman, Frank Deffeari, and they married. But like Hollywood movie stars, no one, not even Frank, would let her take his last name. Even in the phone book, the listing remained "Ardella Connor, 30 South Shore Drive."

And 30 South Shore Drive was the waterfront home Ardella had bought and paid cash for, as were the series of late-model Cadillac convertibles that over the years adorned its garage.

Ardella ran the Omar Khayyam for seventeen years. She sold the building to the Edgewater Retirement

Community, and opened her new concept, the Poop Deck, on the beachfront.

A few years thereafter, Ardella was unable to beat a bout with cancer. It was a death that Galvestonians like I mourned hard.

Frank has scrapbooks with pictures and newspaper and magazine articles that chronicle Ardella's days on earth. He has never once considered changing his and Ardella's listing in the phone book. It still reads, Ardella Connor, 30 South Shore Drive. And that's as it should be.

When George's Courage Took Him to His First Dance Ever, He Met Mary

When George had to speak, whether it was before a group or just to his best friend, he always had a look on his face like he was ready to cry. His cheeks would even get flushed. He had always behaved that way.

Many of those who knew him were amateur armchair psychologists. They had come to the same conclusion: that behavior, and a lot of other things about George's persona, were the results of his being shy.

By the time he left for college, he was about 5'9" tall and weighed well over 200 pounds. He had thick black hair that he parted on the left. When he was in his ROTC uniform, he looked like the World War II army picture of his dad that was on the table in his family's living room, except the picture of George's dad had been taken sixteen years before.

Before she came into his life, nobody I know could name one girl George had ever dated. And by then he was getting ready to begin his second semester at Texas Tech.

What acumen George lacked in his ability to interact with the opposite sex, he made up for in his ability to drink at one sitting multiple cocktails of Seagram's 7 Crown and Coke. In those days that was an admired trait called, "having built up his tolerance."

It was this time of the year about 1959. One of the Ball High sororities was to have its annual Christmas season dance at the Hotel Galvez's Grecian Room. The number of invitations sent was limited to the most popular, and while the dress was shown on the invitation's lower left corner as semi-formal, if a boy showed up in anything but a tux, he could rest assured he wouldn't be invited the following year, popular or not.

Throughout his high school career, George had never gotten an invitation to a sorority dance. Oddly, this time he had made the list. George waited until the afternoon of the dance to rent a tux. He shined up his black-plastic ROTC shoes. Now dressed up, he began working on building his courage. After several 7-Crowns and Coke, he walked into the Grecian Room as a stag. By then it was after 9 o'clock.

George was not a handsome man, but like every man who has ever inhabited the universe, put him in a tux, and he was worth a second glance.

When he came in, nobody could believe it. Not only had George gotten an invitation, but also he had rented a tux and had the courage to walk in alone. The only thing that now made him different from 200 others was that he was without a date.

Mary was a Ball High senior, and she was one of the graduating sorority members being honored that year. She had been dating a handsome athlete, but on this particular night, he had a monstrous case of infectious mononucleosis, and old Dr. B.R. Parrish had told him he must stay in bed. Mary was at the dance by herself.

When George entered the Grecian Room, the oddest thing happened. Joe Ginsberg's Orchestra began playing its next chart. It was the Johnny Mathis song, "Chances Are."

"Chances are, for I wear a silly grin, the moment you come into view...."

Without so much as a word, Mary got up from the table where she was sitting with friends, walked across the room and met George. Without missing a beat, they began to dance.

Nobody knew George could dance—George probably didn't know he could either. But from that moment, and for the remainder of that night, George and Mary gracefully maneuvered every slow dance. And when they weren't dancing, they were by themselves at a table, talking.

When the night ended, Mary rode home with another couple. George left the way he had come, by himself. But for the remainder of the Christmas holidays, Mary and George were a couple, that was until Mary's sick boyfriend found out. He raised a huge stink.

So on New Year's Eve, Mary went out with her boyfriend, and George, now pouting, went night clubbing. He ended the evening at Lee Woodson's Colony Club on 20th and Strand where there was an after-hours strip show. The star attraction was a girl named Candy with whom he had graduated from high school the year before.

While George was night clubbing that evening, Mary was breaking up with her boy friend. New Year's Day, around noon, Mary called George's home, only to learn from his mother that George hadn't come home the night before. The family was worried. In fact, George's brother had been looking for him since nine that morning.

Mary got in her family's pink and charcoal Crown Victoria, and started looking for George's car. She drove down 25th Street, and when she got to the Southern Union Gas Co. building, she saw a body dressed in jeans lying in a semi-fetal position in the gutter. She recognized the hair. It was George. His hands formed a pillow under his cheek. He was facing the curb. One shoe was on the sidewalk.

She left the Ford in the middle of the street, and ran over to him. Even as inexperienced as Mary was about such things, in a matter of moments she determined he wasn't dead or hurt. She knew he had gotten drunk and passed out in the ditch. His car was nowhere in site. How he had gotten there was as mystery.

Crying hysterically, she began trying to wake up George. Just then a hand touched her shoulder and a deep and comforting voice said to her, "I'm the Rev. M.C. Battles, pastor of Mt. Olive Baptist Church. Let me help you." As far as Mary was concerned, he had come out of nowhere, and he had brought with him the comforting voice of an angel.

Once he had George awake and on his feet, the minister got him into his car. Then he and Mary took George to his church's parsonage. Mary sat in the living room while the pastor led George into the kitchen and closed the door.

About an hour later, the two came out and joined Mary. Within mere moments, the doorbell rang. It was an older man—a man neither George nor Mary knew. After the minister introduced them to the older man, the three men excused themselves and went into the kitchen, leaving Mary alone.

Another hour passed before they came out to join Mary. It was then that Battles told her that the older man was a member of Alcoholics Anonymous, and that George had agreed to let his new friend lead him to a life of sobriety.

When Texas Tech's spring semester started the following week, it did it without George. Instead he, the AA counselor, Mary and the pastor continued working as a team. That three were as rabid about helping George reach his new goal as he was.

When I saw George and Mary in the grocery store last week, Mary said that George has been sober for more than thirty-five years; they have been married for thirty-six. I couldn't help but notice they were holding hands. All of the time we visited, George never once looked like he was going to cry. He had an attractive confidence about him.

George and Mary told me that the fact that he had become sober and remained so is easily explained: It is a matter of George's desire and ability to exercise will power. What is unexplainable, they said, is that George showed up at his first sorority dance in 1959, that he was stag, that Mary's boyfriend was ill, and that a Johnny Mathis song provided such a strong magnetism that it brought two unlikely souls together. From those had come a lifetime of happiness and the personal rewards of two people in love working toward common goals.

Tina, Sammy and Nat "King" Cole's "That Sunday, That Summer"

In the early 1960s, W.K. Leonard, who was the manager of Burton Lumber Co., bought and remodeled Jack O'Toole's old Ciro's Club on Seawall, and renamed it the Petite Room.

That was in the days when turquoise, orange and black were the colors decorators were using. That was in the days when the fronts of classy bars were upholstered in a manner called rolled and pleated, and above the back bars were hung huge mirrors.

Every nice nightclub had plastic leatherette-covered couches and chairs, end tables with lamps, and coffee tables. That motif was known as Danish Modern.

The Petite Room looked just like that, and it was very definitely snazzy. Its jukebox even had the music that had been selected by Louise Bird's Pirate Club's bartender, Norris Ellis. Norris' taste in popular and jazz music was as impeccable as it was legendary—lots of Kenton, Dinah Washington, June Christy and Ella, with Spike Jones' "Cocktails for Two" thrown in for laughs.

Leonard hired a young beauty with auburn hair, Jerry Wollard and her new husband, a longshoremen's union bookkeeper named Doug, to manage his new club.

Just after lunch one summer Sunday, the afternoon bartender, Tina, opened the club. Within moments the doorbell rang. When she looked through the peephole, she saw the most handsome fellow she had ever seen. But she didn't know him, and she started to not let him in. After all, Texas law made it illegal to sell liquor by the drink to anyone who was not a member of the club. This guy could be a TLCB man, she thought.

But all of a sudden at that very moment, and without having been primed with so much as a thin dime, the jukebox mysteriously began playing a Nat "King" Cole record.

If I had to choose just one day,
To last my whole life through,
It would surely be that Sunday.
The day that I met you.

Tina knew she had never heard the song before, wasn't sure when Norris had put it on the jukebox, and surely didn't know why it was playing then. So she took it in sum total as an omen that had something to do with the handsome young man whom she was looking at through the peephole. After all, this was Sunday like the song said. She let him in.

The afternoon was slow, so Tina and her customer began chatting, and he began buying her a cocktail every time he bought himself one. Before long, she was sitting on the barstool next to him, and he had told her his name was Sammy.

When Jerry came in at seven to relieve her, Tina and Sammy decided to go to the Pirate Club for an Oscar steak. They continued to get along marvelously, and before too many days had passed, they were going steady.

One Saturday night Tina was bartending and Jerry was hostessing when the doorbell rang. It was Tina's boyfriend, and he was in some sort of rage about her cheating on him with another man.

No amount of talking and testifying by Tina and Jerry was going to change his mind and settle him down. About that time, Doug came in.

Doug was a 1940s Sinatra-size man who wore black-rimmed, green-lensed sunglasses day and night, and had big shoulder pads in his suit coats. If you looked closely, you could tell he also wore Elevator shoes. But he looked mean enough that no one ever messed with him. Sammy didn't either, as Doug bounced him out the front door.

Later that night, as nightclub people used to do after closing hours, Tina, Doug and Jerry went to the Pirate Club for a nightcap and to unwind. In the back door came Sammy, waiving a 38 snub-nose and threatening to kill Tina. That kind of foolishness never set will with Louise Bird, so she took the gun away from him and threw him out.

Louise Bird was like a modern day "Gun Smoke's" Miss Kitty. She was elegant and always a lady. She commanded so much respect from her customers that no one, no matter how mad or drunk, ever made her so much as raise her voice when she wanted them to leave. Sammy didn't either

Weeks past and no one saw Sammy. He didn't call, he didn't write, and he didn't send flowers or a card to Tina. There was no apology.

Then one Sunday afternoon in early August, Tina opened the club after lunch. She put a red quarter in the jukebox, selected six songs, and the first one to come up was that Nat "King" Cole tune. Wouldn't you know the doorbell rang, and when she looked through the peephole, it was Sammy? Just like before, she took it as an omen, and let him in.

He said he was sorry, she fixed him an Old Forester "up" with a water back, and they began to dance.

Newborn whippoorwills were calling from the hills
Summer was a-coming in but fast.
Lots of daffodils were showing off their skills—
Nodding all together I could almost hear them whisper,
"Go on, kiss him, go on and kiss him."

So she did, and then she began quietly singing the song's confession in Sammy's ear.

If I had to choose one moment,
To live within my heart,
It would be that tender moment
Recalling how we started.
Darling, it would be when you smiled at me
That way, that Sunday, that summer.

Within a few weeks thereafter, Judge Jimmy Piperi married Sammy and Tina, and they moved to a house they had rented on the mainland.

One Monday afternoon, Tina came home early from work, and when she walked into the house, she found Sammy on the couch with another woman, a woman who, unbeknownst to Tina was Sammy's sister. Without saying so much as a word, Tina pulled out of her purse a 25-caliber pistol, the pistol Sammy had given her for protection, and she shot Sammy dead.

That Monday was February 15, 1965. It was the same Monday that Nat "King" Cole passed away after a long bout with lung cancer.

Humor

The Elements of Style

Heber Taylor of "The Daily News" and I were discussing style. He said I ought to write about it. I suggested if that were a subject near and dear to his heart, he should allot one of his columns to it. I'd rather tell stories, I said. He kept on with what was his idea of a convincing argument. Not that it was all that good, actually, but that he authorizes my monthly check had a way of ameliorating my desire to put forth a counter-proposal.

Heber Taylor

Perhaps I could trick him into being more realistic if I used the "I will, if you will," tactic. I figured he'd far rather pen more thoughts about something the Wise Woman had said to him, to again prove her to be his intellectual superior. Since he didn't respond, I thought I had him. But three days later his column on style appeared in the paper. Here's my offering on the subject of style.

I'd say without hesitation that my daddy, well-bred

and educated Kentucky gentleman William Wallace Cherry, had more overall style than anyone I've ever known. You'd find few, if any, who knew him who would take exception to that evaluation.

In 1954, Jim Bradner gave me a job at KGBC as a teenage disc jockey. Wanting to look successful and grown up, I took my first paycheck and bought two white dress shirts with French cuffs from my surrogate uncle Julian at E.S. Levy's and had the pockets hand-monogrammed in maroon with my initials, WSC.

It was then that my daddy explained to his fourteen year old son how monograms can contribute to or detract from a man's style.

"First, only a shirt that has been custom tailored should be monogrammed, and then the monogram should be placed four inches above the waist, and four inches in front of where the left arm naturally hangs. And further, if you're a man who is important enough to have a custom made, monogrammed shirt, it must be without a pocket," he said.

"The man who wears that shirt has no need for a shirt pocket," he went on to explain with a twinkle in his eye, "because with that amount of position, he most certainly has an assistant who is walking three steps behind him, and it is the assistant who is the one carrying his pen and note pad. And further, with that shirt, he wears braces matching the monogram's stitching, and never, ever a belt."

After a lifetime of lessons on style by William Wallace Cherry, I'm not sure whether or not I actually have any, but I will promise you I am an authority on evaluating when it exists and when it doesn't. I now put forth these examples for your consideration.

In the main, the female gender in its entirety looks terrible in anything made of leather other than shoes. Joan McLeod and her daughter, Joanie, are the exceptions. If you will look as good in leather skirts, slacks and blouses as either of them do, fine. If not, clothes made of wool, silk and cotton are still your best bet.

People, in general, show lack of style when they cuss. The exception is Ruth Kempner. When she uses a four letter word, it is with great style. No minister who cusses can do it with style, so ministers shouldn't ever cuss. You probably shouldn't either unless you think you can do it with Kempner's flair. Even then, it's highly questionable you'll attain that goal. Best to not chance it.

Stay away from convertibles. Dr. Edward and Nonie Thompson, Harris Kempner and Francis K. Harris are the only people I ever saw who exhibited style when they drove their convertibles, save and except their antithesis, the flashy gamblers from the Island's past like Joe Pajucie.

Flat-top caps look good on some men, but on most they don't. Andy Morgan is an exception. He has worn a flat-top cap for the forty-five years I've known him. Andy Morgan's cap and his excellent speaking voice are testaments to his great style.

Chanel No. 5 gives an aroma of style to every woman who wears it; most of the other perfumes don't. Royall Lyme and Royall Spyce are excellent scents for

Galveston Memories

men; Polo, Halston and the like aren't and never were. Fabrege Aphrodisa was in 1956. Bay Rum and Old Spice were anytime before 1954. Jeris Hair Tonic never was, nor was Vitalis.

Restaurants without cloth tablecloths, cloth napkins and full silver services for each guest are without style. Restaurants in which the first words spoken to the guests is the run-on sentence, "I'm-Jennifer-and-I'll-be-your-server-tonight-give-me-your-drink-orders-so-I-can-go-get-them-started-before-I-take-your-order," have no earthly concept of the noun, "style." Further, please tell me what "so I can go get them started" means.

New restaurants and bars designed and furnished by Amber Felts have great style. Those done by others probably don't. Events staged by Harry Rice are sure to have great flair and style.

I once complained to Harris Kempner about the newly redecorated Artillery Club. "I quit worrying about that long ago," he said. "The next president's wife will redecorate it just as badly. Most of those thereafter will as well. Focus on savoring your martini. It is tradition here that the president's wife will have nothing to do with making them."

Matt Doyle once told me that his dad, then Texas City Mayor Chuck, spit polished his shoes and those of his children every Saturday in preparation for Sunday Mass. The combination of the polished shoes and a family going to church together each week shows Chuck Doyle has style.

Dining room tables set with an assortment of the family silver patterns from the past have great style.

Beginning in the late 50s, Ardella Connor wore a harem outfit and a jewel in her belly button. Few women who ever inhabited this island had as much style as Ardella. None had more. Ardella owned the Omar Khayyam Club.

There are big houses, small houses, expensive houses and not so expensive houses in Galveston. The one with the greatest exhibition of a stylish flair is at 2521 Winnie.

Twenty-fifth Street has a chance of having a smidgen of style; Broadway has none.

Mercedes sold countless two-seater roadsters. Only four people ever exhibited style by driving one: Margy Kelso, Leroy Brown, Sandy Cherry and one other person whom I passed on the highway once, but I don't recall that I knew him.

Maggies and Escentials on the Strand are two shops with great style. When La Kings Confectionery gets a couple of more years of wear, it has a good chance of having style, too. In its heyday, the Star Drug Store had style, from top to bottom. The Old Strand Emporium has style, but it wouldn't if it didn't have Bill and Karen Fullen.

When Ira Berry reached his eightieth birthday, those in Buddy Benson's mother's rooming house where Mr. Berry took his meals said, "What do you think about being eighty, Mr. Berry?" Berry answered in his always proper Shakespearean actor diction, "I like it fine. You have a lot less chance of dying when you are eighty than you do when you are seventy." Ira Berry and his wit had great style.

Attorney Sherwood Brown, Jr., told stories. Few ever got their point. As Judge Jerome Jones pointed out when he gave Brown's eulogy, it didn't matter. Brown got so tickled telling the story, that his own laughter made it worthwhile to the listener. Sherwood Brown's laughter had great style.

Late 50s Turf Grill cashier and U.S. National Bank Barber Shop manicurist Melba (Toast) had great style just for being Melba Toast.

The 1999 Lincoln is the first American automobile to have design style in more than twenty-five years. It is difficult to drive this car and not exude auto ownership style.

Sanibel Island, Florida has style. It is Galveston done right. To cross the bridge to the island you pay a fee; your leave costs nothing. The first time a person litters, overparks or speeds, he gets a friendly warning. If he does it again, he is fined at which time he is also evaluated by the authorities as possibly being on a crime wave. His behavior is then carefully monitored by both the authorities and his neighbors; in fact, so much so that he either gets with the program, or he moves.

Galveston would be wise to emulate Sanibel Island rather than follow its current course. The first step would be the easiest. Its official name needs to be Galveston Island, Texas. The rest of the formula is merely a matter of having and displaying Attitude with a capital "A."

1909: Young Men's Progressive Association Opens Model Laundry

Sam Farb

Sam Farb told me many years ago that a man is foolish if he goes into a business he knows nothing about. My friend Alan Rudy's advice was one should never invest in land until he has a use for it. And then my dad told me to never own stock in a business whose assets eat. I tested all three of these for accuracy, and can assure you that on all accounts the advice was correct.

Octogenarian Charles Kilgore, who has spent his entire life in League City, relayed this story to me, told him by Chris Tellefson who owned the Interurban Queen Newsstand.

Around 1908, a group of young men who partied together, did so under an impressive sounding name, Young Men's Progressive Association. Somewhere along the way, they decided that their group needed to have a civic purpose. It was decided the club would establish a "war chest" and that dues and assessments would go into that treasury.

The group then charged itself with figuring out what important business was missing in Galveston. From that point forward, "their meetings were dominated with long discussions on what kind of venture or facility the city needed," Kilgore went on to explain.

"The war chest continued to grow. The weekly discussions continued about what to spend it on. The final decision became apparent. What was required for Galveston to truly be a progressive city was for it to have a modern laundry," Kilgore said Tellefson had told him.

There were many laundries on the Island in those days, but they were primarily Chinese laundries, laundries that were no more than a family taking in wash, doing it in wash tubs, hanging it outside on clothes lines to dry, ironing it, then delivering it back to the customers.

The Young Men's Progressive Association picked one of its most popular members who was a well-known community leader, to head the new operation that would be called the Model Laundry. A fine two-story brick building was built at the corner of 25th and Church streets, and it was filled with the most modern equipment. All in all, the Model Laundry's facilities were the best money could buy.

Special horse-drawn wagons were built, for after all top service was also their goal, and that required free home pick-up and delivery.

A great deal of advertising was done, and because the members of the Young Men's Progressive Association

Galveston Memories

were so well-known throughout the city, the day the Model Laundry opened for business, all of the laundry wagons came in loaded to the top with bags of soiled clothes. The YMPA was sure they had a success on their hands.

Each customer's bag came with a laundry list with Model Laundry printed at the top—4 white shirts, 12 celluloid collars, 17 men's handkerchiefs, 2 pair pajamas, 12 pair socks, 4 sheets, 8 pillowcases, 6 women's blouses, 2 bonnets, etc.

In addition to the hired employees, there was no question that to get the business off the ground on the first day, the members of the YMPA were going to have to work in the laundry plant as well. They brought in food and liquor. They might as well have a victory celebration along with their opening day labor, they reasoned.

Everything was going fine. For the most part, the machinery washed the clothes well, and the big coal burning dryers did their job, and then the irons that were attached to the huge steam boilers beautifully finished the flat work and shirts. Even the non-ironed pieces, called "fluff-dry" looked almost as if they had been pressed, after they had been neatly folded.

Everything was going well until it was time to wrap the laundry in the Kraft paper, reload it back in the route wagons, and send it out to the customers. It was then that for the first time the management and the owners of the Model Laundry realized that they had no earthly idea what specific garments belong to which specific customers.

"None of the committee knew how to mark clothes—hadn't even thought about it until then," Kilgore said. So with the very limited information they had—the customers' laundry lists—they tried to send back to each client the specific number of socks, shirts, handkerchiefs, sheets and pillowcases that was on the customer's laundry list. However, if any of a customer's own garments turned up in the package, it was just luck.

Even that didn't work all of the time. "If you had sent in two pair of socks, it was entirely possible you got back two pair of someone else's drawers," Kilgore said.

It didn't take long for the men of the YMPA to entertain a motion, a second and have it pass by acclamation. The following day, the Model Laundry went out of business and was placed on the market for sale. None of this would have happened had they had and followed the advice of Sam Farb.

In 1910, six investors bought the Model Laundry Corp. from the men of the YMPA. The five operating stockholders were W.A. Johnson, Charles J. Michaelis, C.M. Hess, F.L. Coffey and Wilbur Goodman.

The Model Laundry operated continuously until only one of the original stockholders was left, Wilbur Goodman. All the others had died, one by one. Goodman sold it in 1970, when he was eighty-three years old.

As for Charles Kilgore, he has spent his entire life in League City. He worked in his family's lumber business, which his father started as a general store on April 18, 1915. The Kilgores sold the business seventy years later. By then its annual sales exceeded $15 million. Now eighty-two, Charles Kilgore has a second success on his hands, a real estate business. He closes each business day at exactly 5 p.m., celebrating with a Scotch.

Kilgore's ties to Galveston are strong. His cousins were Bob and Cecile Chambers, former owners of what is now called the Grover-Chambers House on Market Street. "It was shelled by the Yankees during the Battle of Galveston," Kilgore reminded me.

"Yeah, and Grover didn't fight in the war because he had a bum arm," I reminded Kilgore, just to show him I'm not a neophyte on Island history.

Charles Kilgore

Galveston's Twin Foondinis, the Inspiration for Las Vegas' Siegfried and Roy?

Some think it is possible that Siegfried and Roy, the famous Las Vegas magic duo, got their inspiration to work as a team, rather than as singles, from a Galveston act of the early 1950s known as the "Twin Foondinis."

After all, other than the Twin Foondinis, few if any can think of one famous magic act, even as far back as Harry Blackstone and the days of vaudeville before him, where a magic team shared equal billing on the marquee.

The Twin Foondinis were of midget size. Although one was slightly taller than the other was, neither broke the five-foot mark. When they performed, they dressed in over-sized tuxedos and theatrical black moustaches glued on with Dentyne rather than spirit gum.

While I've heard it said that their baggy tuxes were for the purpose of hiding from the audience the extra playing cards and the white doves, the truth is the Foondinis then were not of sufficient fame and means to afford tailor-made formals from Frank and Blanche Ortiz's Ace Tailors. The Foondinis made do with what they could borrow from relatives.

In order to put their first magic act together, the Foondinis spent hours evaluating the tricks that were taught by how-to books from the Rosenberg Library. Lots of them could be done with Bicycle cards and items available around the house. With the help of librarian Miss

Emma Lee, the Foondinis built up a wonderful repertoire of mystifying illusions.

But they also knew they needed some real showstoppers. Fortunately, every comic book of the day carried a full-page ad for Johnson Smith Co. of Detroit. And while it was the company's whoopee cushions, joy buzzers and red-hot pepper gum for which it was most famous, it also stocked a variety of supplies for magicians—even magic wands, top hats and consecutively numbered and rolled show tickets.

Without going into debt, the Foondini twins were able to buy four very special tricks plus one top hat and one magic wand. One of tricks was the famous ball-and-vase illusion, a slight-of-hand trick that the catalog said had "never failed to astonish an audience" during the forty years it had been featured.

The date for the first Galveston show was set for a Saturday afternoon in April. But as the time began running short, the team's advance man, who was one of the younger Foondini brothers, walked off the job in a fit of rage, and that left the Twin Foondinis at the last minute responsible for doing their own promotion.

With a hand-cranked printing press and colored construction paper, on the Friday before the show, handbills were printed and distributed under the windshield wiper blades of the cars parked at C.P. Evans Food Store on 45th and Avenue S.

In exchange for four free tickets to the performance, professional sign painter Maurice Hennessy designed and painted a large show card with lots of sparkle glued on it, and with a devilish looking rabbit peeking out of a black top hat. A magic wand was shown lying nonchalantly by its side.

The sign announced that the Twin Foondinis would be holding "one performance and one performance only," in the unused quarters adjacent to the garage of a house on Sherman Drive.

In addition to the Twin Foondinis, Hennessy's other famous clients included the Balinese Room and Richard Bovio and the Merrymakers.

The day and time arrived, and by peaking through the crack between the stage curtains, the Twin Foondinis saw that the house was packed. They marveled at their good fortune. Apparently many of their relatives had been shopping at Evans when the handbills were put under car wiper blades. They had all come. In fact, there were nearly thirty people in the audience. Six of those filled the small "standing room only" section.

Even Paul Bergan, director of music for GISD and Galveston's most famous illusionist had come out of his respect for these talented men of the profession. The young people's minister from the Westminster Presbyterian Church and his fiancée were also among those in the audience.

The Twin Foondinis brought gasps, awes and applause as they adroitly went through their repertoire of audience-mystifying illusions. It all built to the finale, the famous ball-and-vase slight of hand illusion. So stunting was the climax that it brought the audience to its feet while the sounds of their wild clapping and loud cheers and whistles resonated from the walls.

Galveston Memories

With that, bows were taken, the curtain closed, and the Twin Foondinis took seats at the reception table to sign autographs. Afterwards, the audience moved to the backyard gardens for early evening popcorn, punch and a series of 8-mm film cartoons.

But much to the disappointment of future audiences everywhere, and even in light of that grand success, the Twin Foondinis never again performed. Nevertheless, their legendary performance lives on.

In the fall of 1953, it was charged by some local fame-jealous Walter Winchell type that "Foondini" was, in fact, a nom de plume, and further, that the magicians were not only not twins, but weren't even brothers. They were just friends who happened to be both dark-headed and short.

But it wasn't until just before Halloween in 1997, that one of the Foondinis finally spilled the beans, and admitted that under one of the Foondini disguises had been he, Jasper E. Tramonte. To this day, however, no one has ever learned the name of the other member of Galveston's famous illusionist duo, the duo that is thought to be the inspiration for the team of Siegfried and Roy, Galveston's great prestidigitators, the renowned Twin Foondinis.

Left to right: (1955) Jasper E. Tramonte, Peggy Mayo, Bandleader Billy Williams, Patricia McInerney, Bill Cherry

It Took a Fire at the Laundromat for the World to Learn Crawford's Secret

Everyone called her "Crawford." I don't think I ever heard her first name. The old timers who I called to check out my recollection of this story said they only knew her as "Crawford," too.

She had been in the military during the Korean Conflict, and had served along with the medics. And that's why Crawford was in Galveston. She felt sure that in the service she had found her calling. She was studying nursing.

Crawford was nearly 5'9" in her stocking feet. She had dark-chestnut hair, haunting green eyes, and full lips. And if the season allowed, be assured her skin was tanned and the air around her smelled wonderful—the fragrance of Coppertone suntan lotion and beach sand.

In the summer, you'd find her in a two-piece bathing suit or tight white shorts and a red and white, stripped tee shirt. Winters, it was a straight skirt with a kick pleat and a tight sweater. When someone needed good-looking girls to model in a photograph, more often than not, Crawford was in the group.

And the medical students, the young lawyers and bankers, and the various single engineers who worked in Texas City but lived on the island, all but stood in line to date her. She made it a point to not get serious about any of them. You rarely saw her twice with the same fellow, and that was her choosing, not theirs. Back then they called girls like Crawford "sirens."

It was a cold Sunday afternoon in January, and Crawford and some of her girlfriends had decided to spend the afternoon washing their clothes at the laundromat. They figured they'd put their wash into the big stainless steel front-loading Bendix washing machines, then stay there and read cheap paper-back novels until theft clothes were finished.

That plan lasted until they had loaded up the clothes dryers, packing them as tight as they could with the hopes two quarters each would dry everything. After all, that bought them a full hour on the machine's timer.

There was a fellow named Sommers who had a red 49 Ford convertible, and since the top had some tears in it he'd patched with electrician's tape, unless it was raining a downpour, you'd see him driving with the top down, summer and winter. Sommers was a nice-looking fellow with straight sandy hair, who was happy with his public reputation for being a ladies' man. He had recently graduated from Sam Houston on the GI Bill, and was a public school teacher.

Sommers was cruising around town with five of his friends, when he spotted Crawford's Crosley parked in front of the laundromat. He pulled in, and they got out and went inside. After some chitchat, Sommers convinced

Crawford and her three friends that while their clothes were drying they should all go to the Jack Tar's Coffee Cove for hot chocolate. He was buying.

Since there were nine of them, it would take two of the booths with a chair pulled up to the end of one of them for the Coffee Cove to seat them as a group. You would have laughed if you could have been there and seen Sommers trying to jockey his position so he could sit in the booth next to Crawford. All the while Crawford had her eye on one of Sommers' friends, and, of course, she was trying to sit next to him. But Sommers was an expert, so he won the unspoken contest.

The two booths-full had been at the Coffee Cove for about forty-five minutes when they heard the sirens and the roars of what sounded like a full symphony of fire trucks coming toward them. The trucks stopped not far away. One of Sommers' friends insisted that they pay the bill, and go see the fire.

When they got outside, the winter air smelled like burning rubber. As soon as they started down 6th Street from the Boulevard, they saw the fire trucks were parked in front of the laundromat and bellows of smoke were coming out its door. Sommers and Crawford parked their cars on the street, and all ran to the parking lot in front of the laundromat.

By then a crowd had developed, and Crawford and the girls, and Sommers and the boys, realized they couldn't do anything more than join it. The girls, of course, started their own private, silent prayer vigils with the hopes that would keep the dryer that was on fire from being one of theirs.

Within about ten minutes, the firemen had the situation under control, and the smoke inside the building was clearing. It was then that Crawford saw a fireman open the door of the dryer she was sure her clothes were in. She covered up her face with her hands.

The fireman walked out of the door of the laundromat and onto the parking lot, held up a handful of very large, partially burned and otherwise charred foam rubber padded bras and yelled to the crowd, "Anyone here named Crawford? We need to write a report."

Just before Crawford had left for her first year of nursing school, her mother had thoughtfully tacked cloth name tags in all of her daughter's clothes. There was no way Crawford could deny the fire had been in her dryer. Now the secret she had so carefully guarded was public information.

Champ's European Shopping Spree Turned Out to Be a Mistake

He was tall, skinny, and had hairless pasty-white legs with e was tall, skinny, and had hairless pasty-white legs with knobby knees. His face was full of reddish freckles. I think his nickname was Champ.

There were only a few swimming pools in Galveston in the 50s. Aside from the ones at the Galveston Country Club, the YMCA, the Elks Club and the Knights of Columbus, if you were going to swim some place other than in the gulf, the chances were your family had to have a swimming club membership at one of the beach front e e e was tall, skinny, and had hairless pasty-white legs with knobby knees. His face was full of reddish freckles. I think his nickname was Champ.

There were only a few swimming pools in Galveston in the 50s. Aside from the ones at the Galveston Country Club, the YMCA, the Elks Club and the Knights of Columbus, if you were going to swim some place other than in the gulf, the chances were your family had to have a swimming club membership at one of the beach front hotels.

Champ's family were members of the Galvez Club.

Galveston Memories

When Champ graduated from high school, his family bought him a two week tour of Europe. As he went through the various countries, just like every other tourist, he bought the legendary costumes.

He got wooden shoes in Holland, argyle knee socks in Scotland, and one of those green Robin Hood hats with the long orange feather in it from Finland. He bought a pair of lederhosen (those short pants with the suspenders) in Germany, and a big-bowled smoking pipe with a curved stem in London.

When he got back to Galveston, he decided to put on the whole getup at once, and go cruise the Galvez's pool. His dad had given him permission to take the 49 dark-green Studebaker.

Champ reasoned that surely at least one of the Houston girls there would find him fascinating, and if his luck were really good, maybe that evening she would go with him to the Oleander Drive-In for a horror movie, a bag of real-buttered popcorn and some smooching.

Let me stop right here and parenthetically say that Champ could have offered any girl on earth a free shopping spree at Nathan's, and even then he would have had no takers. And one more thing: No girl on this planet ever went smooching with any boy whose wheels were his father's 49 Studebaker, even if he were Frankie Avalon, so this idea was doomed from the start.

Well, the pool was filled with teenage boys swimming, doing cannon balls from the diving board, and making noise. And in every lounge chair there was a girl, getting sun, and hoping the homemade suntan solution of Johnson's Baby Oil and iodine from C & S Drugstore would make her skin golden brown. Beside each chair was a portable tube radio tuned to KILT, when one could have easily served the whole area.

About then, out of the hotel lobby door came Champ, clomping along in his wooden shoes, with his green felt Robin Hood hat, the orange feather waving in the breeze, and puffing up a storm on his Sherlock Holmes pipe. His goofy hairless legs with the knobby knees were spanning the distance between the wooden shoes and the lederhosen.

He had a big smile on his face, his left hand wrapped around the pipe bowl just like he'd seen it done in the movies. He was sure he was, for the very first time, the envy of the crowd.

But just as you are thinking right now, the thought that was coming into everyone's mind but Champ's, even those who were just inches away from sainthood, was that Champ needed to be drowned in that pool. Fortunately for Champ the lifeguard on duty was Kirwin's Coach Aubry Baker, and everyone knew he wouldn't stand for a drowning on his watch.

About that time, Champ saw a Bellaire kid he knew named Levy. Champ yelled at him, "As we say in German, how's your daddy's s----- business?" Here he tried to pronounce the German word for "tool." The problem was that Levy thought he had used a Yiddish word that sounds similarly, but means something you don't say in polite company.

Out of the pool came Levy, all the while throwing a

fit and falling in it. He got a good hold on Champ and heaved him into the pool. Then Levy went in after him. They wrestled around in there for a while, and finally Champ got loose.

By now the green dye from the Robin Hood hat was running down Champ's face. One wooden shoe had floated off, the other was stuck on his right foot because the wood had swollen. For some reason Champ still had the pipe grasped between his teeth although by then the tobacco was surface scum on the water.

Somehow Champ was able to get out of the pool, and he started to make what he hoped would be a lifesaving get-away. By then everyone watching this scene was doubled up in laughter. Champ was trying to run away with his one wooden shoe on, the other floating upside down in the pool. The foot dressed in just an argyle sock was at least three inches shorter than the one with the wooden shoe. He was holding the Robin Hood hat on with his left hand, and the pipe in his mouth with his right.

Chasing Champ was Levy, yelling in Yiddish one insult after another. Nevertheless, Champ made it from the pool, through the door, and down the long hall to the hotel lobby. Levy was still behind him. A convention bus had just unloaded and the lobby was filled with check-ins.

Of course, no one in there could believe their eyes as Champ, followed by Levy, zoomed by. Remember, here was a kid with skinny, hairless legs in lederhosen, a pipe drooping from his clenched teeth, a face now totally dyed green from the color that had run down his face from the hat with the orange feather in it, clomping along on the tile floor in a syncopated rhythm caused by the alternation of one wooden-shoed foot and one argyle-covered foot.

Behind him was Levy, shirtless, shoeless, wet and in his father's plaid swimming trunks, which I forgot to tell you were too big for him, so he had made them fit by clumping the waistband material into two fist-fulls, one on each side, both held by big brass laundry bag safety pins he had borrowed from the hotel's housekeeping department.

As Champ ran toward the door at the west end of the lobby that would lead him to 21st Street and his chance for a get-away, he prayed that the 49 Studebaker with the drooping headliner, parked at the curb, would start on the first try.

I suppose the good Lord decided Champ had been through enough for one day, for when Champ jumped into the unlocked car, put the key in and pushed the starter, it worked.

As he drove away drove, Levy stood at the curb, still swearing in Yiddish and waving his fist in the air.

As soon as he got home, Champ tossed all of his European trip get-up, except for the pipe, into the garbage can behind the garage. He hoped that by the time summer was over, everyone would have forgotten about that humiliating experience. Probably most did.

But I never pass the Galvez Hotel, like I did today, that I don't think about Champ, his lederhosen, the one wooden shoe, his Robin Hood hat with the orange feather, and the Sherlock Holmes pipe between his teeth, as he was running for his life from Levy, and this June marks forty-three years.

Homer Sechtuals

Mayor George Roy Clough refused to put up with Homer Sechtuals.

Fuqua's Drugstore was on the corner of 39th and Avenue N, and like most drugstores, it had a soda fountain.

Neil Lewis, Denny Doyle, Randolph Parker, and the owner's son, Luther, were among those who worked there as soda jerks. Their take-home pay was $14 a week.

Although the wages weren't much, knowing the drugstore's regular customers, like TV star Utah Carl Beach, former western movie bit-part actor Guitar Ted, newsman Tom Lewis, news photographer Bill Johnson, and mayor George Roy Clough, plus a host of other characters, made the jobs worthwhile.

George Roy Clough had only been Galveston's mayor for a few months when, just before closing-time one night, he came by Fuqua's. He ordered his usual double-thick vanilla malt, and then bragged to the soda jerk and his friends, who were sitting on the last stools, that he was getting ready to stage a huge raid on the public restroom at the foot of the 25th Street at Seawall Boulevard.

"We're gonna arrest Homer Sechtuals," he said. "Because with Homer Sechtuals in there, tourists are afraid to use those public facilities, and I'm not gonna tolerate that."

Mayor George Roy Clough

Just about that time Tom Lewis and Bill Johnson wandered in. Lewis lived upstairs over the drugstore. Johnson had stopped by for coffee as he frequently did. At 10 o'clock, Lewis and Johnson would go on their way to run the police beat for the next day's Galveston Daily News.

Clough said to Lewis and Johnson, but for all to hear, "Here's your scoop for tomorrow's paper, boys. We're getting ready to raid the restroom on 25th and Boulevard, and arrest Homer Sechtuals. You need to be there."

With that, and almost as an afterthought, the mayor turned to the soda jerk on duty and invited him and his friends to go along. In fact, he said he'd be glad to take them there and back in his car. Now that presented a very delicate situation for the boys.

You see, Mayor Clough had a green Packard, and of all the cars on earth, the only thing more uncool than a green Packard was a green Studebaker. On the other hand, Lewis had a circa 1952 MG Roadster convertible. It was black with red leather interior, and it had a powerful sounding exhaust system. Its status was the antithesis of the Packard. There was no cooler set of wheels.

The boys wanted to ride with Lewis, but they knew that wasn't going to happen. Lewis, a bachelor in those days, wasn't about to endanger his status with the girls by being seen with his classic MG loaded up with teenage boys.

Fortunately the soda jerk had a 1947 yellow Willys Jeepster convertible, and while it wasn't particularly cool, it certainly was far ahead of the green Packard. The boys decided they'd go in it. The green Packard led the way.

Within moments of the caravan's arrival, police cars, with sirens blaring and emergency lights blinking, came from everywhere. They shut down 25th Street around the restroom. The policemen, pistols drawn, surrounded the building and waited for their cue from the mayor

It was a summer week night, and the Pleasure Pier, which was where the Flagship Hotel is today, was operating full swing. When the pedestrians, as well as the driving traffic, heard and saw all of the police commotion, everything stopped, and everyone's full attention became focused on that restroom building. A big crowd gathered on the nearby sidewalks.

The great Count Basie Orchestra was playing "April in Paris" on the Pleasure Pier's public address system. It could be heard for blocks away as the south breeze pushed the sound waves of the baritone sax section northward.

When all were in place, Mayor Clough, with his electronic bullhorn, climbed out of his green Packard, took his position in front of the police and announced through the bull horn, "This is your mayor speaking. I'm addressing you on behalf of the fine citizens of the city of Galveston, Texas. Homer Sechtuals, come out with your hands up!"

There was a long pause. Nothing happened. Tension began building. Bill Johnson had his big Speed Graphic press camera focused so that when Homer Sechtuals walked out of the door, Johnson could set off the flash and capture for tomorrow's edition, Homer looking dangerous, coming out of the door with his hands up.

Still nothing happened. The great Count Basie Orchestra finished "April in Paris," where upon the Count yelled for a reprise, "One more time . . . one more time . . . one more time," and the band again struck up the song's final bars.

Clough took Basie's triple "One more time," command as his cue, too, and he again demanded, "As the mayor of the fine city of Galveston, Texas, I'm ordering you, Homer Sechtuals, to come out with your hands up.

Within five maybe ten seconds the Basie song was over and the P.A. system went quiet. The crowd was quiet, too.

Then out of the men's side of the restroom wobbled one lone man. He was a million-year-old wino, and was supporting himself with a crutch under his left arm. His right arm was extended so as to hold his hand high above his head. The boys from the drugstore couldn't believe their eyes. How could Homer Sechtuals, obviously a million-year-old wino on a crutch, be a threat to any one?

The crowd on the sidewalks began to laugh. The drivers of the forty or so cars at the Pier Drive-In started honking their horns and blinking their headlights. Frankly, I'd say that within moments the crowd became all but rowdy.

I have no idea as to why, but the Pleasure Pier's P.A. then played Tennessee Ernie Ford singing, "Nearer My God to Thee."

Without saying a word, the mayor took that as his cue, walked over to the green Packard, got inside, and drove off into the night. Lewis put on his leather driving cap, climbed into the MG while Johnson got into his rusted-out Ford, and they went downtown to the police station to capture real news for the next day's paper.

Homer Sechtuals wasn't handcuffed, much less arrested. In fact he was last seen that very night walking north on 25th Street into the darkness. The police left empty-handed.

There was one positive outcome from this event, however. The boys from Fuqua's Drugstore had yet another confirmation, that even with a take-home pay of only $14 a week, they had the best jobs on the planet earth.

Blackie's New Rug and Veralee's Solution to the Problem

Even though Blackie was his nickname, those who knew him found it next to impossible to believe that he had once had jet-black hair that he had worn in a trademark pompadour, because by this time, just approaching fifty, he was totally bald.

Blackie was on his second marriage, and her name was Veralee. She was one of the best beauty operators in Galveston in those days. Blackie made and spent big money.

Bars had to be private clubs in order to make some attempt to comply with the state liquor laws. Hidden next to Ed Wheeler's Busy Bee Cleaners at 43rd Street and Avenue S was Dorothy Graham's small and intimate Metropole Club.

Blackie and Veralee liked to go there just after work for a toddy. So did then Chief of Police Willie Burns and attorney Sherwood Brown, Jr. Sometimes George Bushong dropped by and entertained before his gig at Lloyd's.

Somewhere along the way, Blackie began giving a lot of thought to the fact that he was approaching fifty, and while he was an extremely charming and gracious man, he felt the lack of hair was a true burden.

So one evening he arrived at the Metropole before Veralee, and he had a full head of black hair in the pompadour that he had had when he was in his early twenties. Everyone was shocked. Even Veralee had never seen him with hair.

Willie Burns grinned and said, "My God, Blackie, at least you could have given us the weekend to forget you're bald!"

Well about the time the joking quieted down, Veralee arrived and everyone soon learned that Blackie had not taken her into his confidence that he was going to get a mail-order rug. When she saw it, she wasn't the least bit happy or impressed, and she let him and everyone know it. Even Ed Wheeler at the Busy Bee said he had clearly heard her comments through the wall.

That didn't discourage Blackie. Every time you saw him thereafter, he had on the toupee.

As you might have suspected by now, the rug wasn't all that Blackie had in mind. He also thought he ought to get himself a girlfriend, one younger than Veralee. So it wasn't long thereafter that one evening after he and Veralee had been to the Metropole for their early evening toddy for the body, Blackie returned with new-to-town, redheaded, young and quite frankly, gorgeous Tina on his arm. Everyone was shocked.

They had barely taken seats at a cozy table when the doorbell rang. Dorothy Graham answered it, and in walked Veralee. Without breaking cadence, she walked over to Blackie, jerked the rug off of his head, went into the ladies' room, at which time everyone heard the toilet flush. Out of the restroom she came, and walked over to Sherwood, who was sitting in an easy chair reading the Wall Street Journal with an ever present Scotch and water at his side.

"You're representing me, Sherwood. Draw up the divorce papers tomorrow," Veralee said firmly. The door flew open and she was gone. I mean no more than two minutes had passed from her entrance to her exit.

Almost as quick as Blackie had entered his midlife crisis, it was over. He was bald again, Tina had left him for a younger man, and Veralee's divorce from him was final. Blackie returned to being the old Blackie everyone had known and loved, except this time single.

Nettie Always Shot Them in the Neck

McBride's was a department store on Galveston's Postoffice Street and like most department stores did then, it had a luncheonette.

The store was owned by Galveston's famous matriarch Mary Moody Northen's husband, E.C. Northen. We're talking about 1925.

Kendall ran the luncheonette by day and drank heavily by night. His wife's name was Nettie, she was half American Indian and half Irish, and the Irish part caused her to never be out of sight of her .25 automatic pistol with the genuine mother of pearl handle. And then there was Kendall's and Nettie's ten-year-old son Chic (Milbourne Augustus Sherborne Evans).

Kendall came home from the luncheonette one evening, long after closing, and more than a little drunk. Without saying so much as an angry word, Nettie went to her purse, got out her .25 automatic pistol and shot him through the neck. Fortunately the bullet went out of the other side and sunk itself deep into the apartment's plaster wall without killing Kendall.

But as you might guess, it wasn't long thereafter that Kendall and Nettie divorced. Chic remained with Nettie.

Still good looking and now in the market for a new husband, Nettie began dating again, and one of her most promising suitors was Frank. In the beginning she and Frank were happy together, but that didn't last, and after they broke up, the next suitor in line was known all over the island as Crazy Joe. He got the Crazy part from his addiction to heroin, although Nettie didn't know that when she started dating him.

Well, when Nettie learned that the true romantic interest of Crazy Joe was heroin and not really she, she broke up with him, and immediately started dating Frank again.

Then one night Nettie and Chic were out with Frank, and they were parked in front of Nettie's house. Chic was asleep in the back seat of Frank's Model A touring car. Frank and Nettie were engaged in a long kiss. All of a sudden and out of nowhere Crazy Joe jumped up on the driver's side of the car and started stabbing Frank in the back through the open window.

He did it seventeen times before Frank could turn loose of Nettie, get the door open and pull Crazy Joe inside with him, Nettie and Chic. Never mind that blood was running everywhere, Frank was mad and he and Joe immediately went into a fist fight inside the car.

Nettie was able to get out, but it wasn't until Frank and Crazy Joe landed on Chic that the boy was able to escape, however, not before "the dope head made a swipe at me with the knife . . . and cut my shirt."

Remember Nettie's .25 automatic pistol, the one with the genuine mother of pearl handle? Well, standing at the curb with Chic, almost matter of factly she took it out of her purse and shot Crazy Joe three times in the neck.

Yelling and screaming because his neck felt like it was on fire, Crazy Joe "took off and ran up to the beach, which was only a few blocks away, where somebody picked him up and took him to the hospital where they removed two of the slugs, but missed one."

Meanwhile, Frank was about to bleed to death from the seventeen stab wounds in his back, so Nettie and Chic drove him to the hospital in the bloody Model A touring car.

Now the procedures of the island's legendary John Sealy Hospital Emergency Room were just being formulated and practiced in 1925. But nevertheless they were enough in place for the staff to put Frank with his seventeen stab wounds and Crazy Joe with two of the slugs in his neck removed, the other still in there somewhere, in the same ward.

Frank was on his stomach with his eyes closed and his head turned to the right when they rolled Crazy Joe in. Frank peaked out of the small slit he made by just barely opening his left eyelid. "My God, there he is again," Frank said to himself in his mind's voice.

Just then the orderly rolled the stretcher past Frank's bed whereupon Frank jumped out of the bed and kicked Crazy Joe, aiming at the easy target the white bandages made. The kick reset the remaining slug in Crazy Joe's neck which then punctured a big artery or something and he started hemorrhaging, and he died right there before the orderly could get the doctor.

Since Nettie was the one who fired the shots in the first place, she was charged with murder. Frank wasn't.

But it didn't matter because Nettie and Frank got one of Galveston's most prominent criminal defense lawyers to represent her, whereupon the attorney got the DA to indict her on first degree murder charges so she could plead self-defense.

But this was all eyewash anyway because nothing was going to happen to Nettie. After all, there was one less dope head on the island as a result, the DA didn't want to try the case, and everyone knew that her attorney could easily persuade any jury to a not guilty verdict. So the case was postponed over and over again for many years until it was finally dismissed.

"Of course it was in all of the papers, so we moved to Houston where I went to work after school for the Double Dip Ice Cream Co. for twelve cents per hour," Chic said in his letter recounting the events that had happened more than seventy years before.

Meanwhile, Kendall remarried and he and his new wife had a daughter, my dear friend Ruthie Evans Laquement, and that's where we are today.

Kendall, Chic and Nettie

Joe Pajucie, His Red Cadillac Convertible and the Four Cheap-Looking Girls

Joe Pajucie's snap-brim grey felt hat covered wavy dyed black hair that was greased tight against his head with Yardley's brilliantine. The aroma of too much Old Spice aftershave choked those near him. This was about 1950, and Joe was sixty if he was a day.

In 1950, people who had tattoos were men in the Navy, and earrings were reserved for women, and for those few men who had crossed the equator. The mark of civility was fine clothes, Chanel No. 5, a Pall Mall cigarette taken from a sterling case, a Santos Cruz martini, and being able to dance a good tango, not that Joe Pajucie would have fit anyone's description of a person of civility anyway.

You see although Pajucie wore the snap-brim grey felt hat, below he couldn't resist including a big gold braceleted watch on his left arm, an enormous gold crucifix on a chain around his neck, his flowered silk shirt unbuttoned three from the top, and a flashy gold ring with a kazillion diamond chips clustered together which, at a respectable distance, looked like a five carat stone. Believe me when I tell you, that ring didn't come from

Phillip A. Kuhn's, although Joe Pajucie swore on "all that was holy" that it did.

And Pajucie liked cheap looking women, lots of them; those who wore too tight white shorts, knit halter tops over Frederick's of Hollywood style strapless bullet bras, ankle bracelets and Carmen Miranda platform straw slides.

He drove a red Cadillac convertible. The Plexiglas back window was ripped out from the day he bought it at Childs Motors, but he figured no one knew that when the top was down.

Let me say now that I don't know a soul who knows where Joe Pajucie lived. The city directory of the time shows no listing, and even with an Italian name like Pajucie, nobody I know claimed kin.

Nevertheless, Pajucie was one of a number of wise guys who cruised the island betting on the nags, cheating at gin and poker, and allegedly banking a half-grand from time to time just after a life was extinguished and the still-warm body dropped off on top of someone else's grave at the city cemetery.

On this particular Friday afternoon, it was one of those Galveston days in early March where the water's calm, the tide's way out, and the air's a clear sixty-five degrees or so.

He loaded up his red Cadillac with four of his girls, all dressed in their tight shorts/halter top uniforms. Naturally the convertible top with the missing Plexiglas rear window was down. Three of the girls were sitting on the trunk deck with their legs hanging over the back seat. The fourth was the only ugly one, and she was in the front cuddled next to Joe Pajucie.

After cruising the beach multiple times, each time honking at Frank Fertitta and John Arenas who were standing on the porch at Murdoch's enjoying a smoke, Pajucie figured he'd better get downtown and make the two past due payments on his Cadillac.

So he said to the girls, "I gotta stop in the bank to do some business, then we'll go to the Turf for turkey mornay and a coupla Southern Selects."

Now wise guys back then were noted for having pockets full of big bills to flash around and tip everyone with. But in order to be able to do that meant that their checking account balances could rarely exceeded middle two figures.

Pajucie knew that if he paid the City National Bank the two payments, it would all but wipe out his bankroll. On the other hand, the tellers had already balanced the day's business. If he gave the bank loan officer a check, that would get him off his back, and surely Joe's weekend gambling winnings would be enough to cover the check on Monday.

There was a parking space right in front of the bank, and Joe and his red Cadillac, the top down and with the four girls clad in too tight white shorts, and halter tops over bullet bras, and ankle bracelets above Carmen Miranda straw platform shoes, pulled right in. Bank officer Arthur Ake was watching the whole scene through the bank's glass door and grinning so big it hurt his chapped lips.

Out of the car came Pajucie. He walked up the steps, went into the bank and with an air of confidence gave Ake the hot check.

Pajucie left and with his girls drove back around the block to the Turf Grill. Luck was with him again, he noted. There was a space in front of Henry's Bookstore, and that was just across the street from the Turf. They all went inside, stopping to chat with Melba "Toast," the hostess, before they went to a booth.

Now while the conversation was going on with Melba Toast, Ake was checking to see if the car payment check would clear. He figured it wouldn't. With suspicion confirmed, Ake called Don Webb and had him send a wrecker to pick up the red Cadillac. Knowing wise guys like a book, Ake told Webb he would find the car parked at the Turf.

When Pajucie and the girls came out, the red Cadillac's parking place was now occupied by Mayor Herbie Cartwright's green Packard. Joe Pajucie knew in his heart what had happened, and he was humiliated. But in any case he made a faint attempt to claim to the girls that the red Cadillac must have been stolen.

With that he hailed a cab, and paid the cabby a five spot to take the girls to the beach. On Monday morning it no longer mattered that Pajucie wasn't listed in the city directory, and that no one claimed to be his kin, for like so many other wise guys had done before him as well as after, he had vanished from the Island.

George Mitchell: The Horatio Alger "Strive and Succeed" Award

George Mitchell

Word had come to his office that George Mitchell was to be honored as a recipient of the famous Horatio Alger "Strive and Succeed" Award at a ceremony to be held the following weekend in California. The award is named after the famous mid-19th century writer of children's novels.

The theme of each Alger story centers around a boy of a poor immigrant family who is recognized by a rich and powerful man who then becomes his mentor. With hard work and his mentor's guidance, the boy grows to be a successful man. That certainly described Mitchell's life.

How to tell Mitchell, as well as the public, that he would be receiving the Alger award was the issue. Finally, a humorous solution was dreamed up and arranged by Mitchell's publicist, Dancie Ware.

Galveston Memories

The Galveston Economic Development Committee met for breakfast each Monday morning at the Tremont House Hotel. Mitchell was a member, and rarely missed a meeting. Ware decided this would be a good place and time to let Mitchell and the public in on the news, so she got a team of Mitchell's friends to assist in the announcement.

First, Frank Incaprera would assemble about six members of the Galveston Beach Band. They would stand on the west side of the hotel's front door and be prepared to play the "Aggie War Hymn" as soon as Mitchell walked out of the door. Mitchell is a famous Aggie.

City Manager Doug Matthews and Mayor Barbara Crews would stand just to the east of the front door, so that when Mitchell came out, and the band stopped playing the "Aggie War Hymn," they could jointly present Mitchell with the notice that he was to receive the Horatio Alger award, and then give him some sort of city parchment in recognition of this outstanding honor. Incaprera would then strike up "For He's a Jolly Good Fellow," and all would go back to business as usual. Five minutes spent at most, start to finish.

Radio newsman Vandy Anderson was to be with Matthews and Crews, microphone in hand, ready to both broadcast over KGBC and record "the few words" Matthews and Crews would direct to Mitchell. The News' reporter, pad in hand, was to the left of Anderson.

Across the street and with wide angle and telephoto lenses, Henry Jackson, cameraman for KHOU-TV, would record the whole event for the evening's news.

Everyone in place, Matthews radioed Chief of Police

Dale Rogers who was parked in a space near 23rd and Broadway. With that, the chief came speeding down 23rd Street with red lights flashing and siren wailing. Screeching around the corner to Mechanic Street, he pulled up in front of the hotel, dramatically letting the lights flash and the siren reverberate between the buildings for a few seconds longer, attracting as much attention as possible.

He then threw open the door, flew out of the patrol car, and ran inside the hotel, whereupon he interrupted the GEDC meeting, telling all that some maniac had just hit Mitchell's new Cadillac. Mitchell must come quickly, Rogers urged.

However, as Rogers was running into the hotel dining room, the GEDC meeting was just ending. It had been listening to a presentation by Jack E. Pratt of Dallas who was trying to convince the committee to support casino gambling here. Like Mitchell, Pratt is bald, athletically built, and about six feet tall. He was dressed in a dark grey suit, white shirt and red and black striped tie. Mitchell frequently dresses like that, too.

While Rogers was telling Mitchell about the alleged big wreck, Pratt was completing shaking hands with the GEDC members, and working his way toward the lobby. Seeing a bald headed man in a suit and of Mitchell's size through the hotel's glass door, coming down the lobby's steps, the appointed "look out" gave the signal for Incaprera to begin the "Aggie War Hymn," And, of course, that was Crews' and Matthews' signal to join Anderson at the KGBC and KHOU microphones for the presentation. Jackson began filming.

Galveston Memories

But out of the door walked Pratt, not Mitchell. A fatal mistake in identity by the lookout. The band stopped playing, the camera stopped filming. Crews, Matthews and Anderson had looks of shock on their faces. The crowd that had assembled surmizing what had happened started screaming with laughter. The band members tried to shield their total humiliation, contemporaneous with each wishing he were somewhere else. The whole thing was starting to resemble a bad Aggie joke.

As he walked out of the front door, however, Jack Pratt paused, smiled, nodded to Crews, Matthews, Anderson and then to the band, and then said loud enough for all to hear, "Nice touch," as if that whole ceremony had been arranged for him. He then walked the short distance to the corner, never looking back, where he disappeared toward the Strand.

When Mitchell came out seconds later, no one was much in the mood to give a repeat performance, but in honor of the man, they did. All, that is, but Dale Rogers. By then he had already gotten in his police car, this time leaving the siren and flashing lights off, and aimed it toward city hall for a fresh start.

George Mitchell in front of Tremont Hotel

The Botched Texas Ranger Raid

For whatever reason, by June the Island's 1949 tourist season was showing all of the components of being one of the most successful it had seen since before World War II, although the economy in the rest of Texas was in the doldrums.

George Olsen's big band, along with comedian Joe E. Lewis, was at the Balinese Room over the Gulf at the Seawall and 21st Street.

Downtown, the Studio Lounge was featuring the impersonations and songs of husband and wife team, Peter Lind Hayes and Mary Healy. In fact, Hayes had a hit at the time for Bing Crosby's Decca Records, "I Got a Girl in Galveston." Hayes and Healy frequently sat in for Arthur Godfrey on his CBS morning radio show.

Galveston attorney Sherwood Brown, Jr., who had "connections" in Austin, learned that Homer Garrison's Texas Rangers were preparing to do a massive raid on the gambling casinos in Galveston. Sherwood called the Turf Athletic Club's Sam Maceo.

Now Louise Bird owned and operated the Pirate Club, a famous supper club in those days located behind the Buccaneer Hotel. For those of you who didn't know her, Louise resembled Houston realtor Martha Turner—jet black hair pulled back in a chignon, designer clothes and all—but Louise was even prettier.

Maceo had Beachcomber Christie Mitchell ask Louise to intercede, because as incongurous as it may seem, Louise and Garrison were friends. Maceo knew that she could defuse the magnitude of Garrison's intensions. Sure enough, Louise worked out this agreement with Garrison: Rather than start with the Balinese Room, the first raid would be at the Western Room, which was on the third floor, above the Studio Lounge, the Turf Grill and Tap Room.

Although itself very opulent, the Western Room was small potatoes in comparison to the B-Room. Breaking up the few machines which were there would be nowhere as costly.

I've got to tell you one more thing. The elevator that took patrons from the lobby to and from the Studio Lounge and Western Room was terribly small, holding six people plus Raymond, the elevator operator. Furthermore, if a snail were racing that elevator, the wise man bet on the snail.

My recollection is that it took somewhere in the neighborhood of five minutes, maybe six, for that elevator to rise two floors, a distance of no more than twenty-five feet. And the elevator's empty cab was always kept at the entrance to the Western Room, so double that time.

On this night, guests in the Studio Lounge had been eating and dancing to the music of Tommy Leatherberry and his combo. Earl Llewellyn had just announced, "Direct from Chicago's Chez Paree, ladies and gentlemen, Peter Lind Hayes and Mary Healy!" It was about 11 o'clock. Although early, a handful were gambling on the next floor in the Western Room.

About that time, in the minuscule first-floor lobby, the receptionist looked up and saw the expected five-member Texas Ranger contingency. The elevator was called. It creeped down to the first floor. Meanwhile, upstairs the staff began hiding all of the gambling machines and tables, finishing in record time.

As Raymond was taking the elevator with the Rangers back up, it stalled between floors. It just broke down through no fault of anyone. One of the Rangers tried but he couldn't get it to resume its ascension either.

They could smell the burned carbon of the motor's brushes, but in a fit of paranoia, the Rangers decided they had been double-crossed. They were furious. One took the ax blade meant for use on the gaming machines and pried open the elevator door.

They then chinned themselves up to the second floor and raced Keystone Cops-esque across the postage stamp size dance floor. Leatherberry's band fired up "The Eyes of Texas." Hayes and Healy looked quizzical but nevertheless took what they thought was their cue and began singing "I've been working on the railroad, all the live long day . . .," which after all, are the lyrics everyone but Texans sing to that tune.

Seeing the first door across the floor, the Ranger leading the pack thought it was surely the door to the stairway which would take them up to the Western Room. He flung it open, and there they were in the ladies' restroom among the matron and two shreeking drunk women, one standing on one leg like a flamingo.

Horrified, the Rangers did a quick about-face, this time heading toward the exit sign which led them to the outside fire escape. Down they went to the alley, and back around the block past Hutchings-Sealy National Bank to their squad cars parked in front.

Forget the small potatoes of the Western Room. They had been humiliated, and that meant they were no longer bound by the Louise Bird agreement.

Within three minutes they pulled up under the Balinese canopy, surprising the doorman as well as the receptionist. Like a well rehearsed school fire drill, though, the doorman called to the back on his phone, and the receptionist hit the button in her booth that set off the red warning light and bell in the back. The employees and guests began making preparations for the arrival.

By the time the Rangers made it down the breezeway and through the showroom to the casino, all they found were guests eating dinner and drinking coffee.

That raid, too, was an absolute disaster. Nothing illegal was discovered. No gaming equipment was found to be chopped up. As the Rangers left in total humiliation, the George Olsen big band played "The Eyes of Texas" for their recessional.

Galveston Memories

Just after midnight the phone rang at the Pirate Club. The operator said, "Person-to-person call for Louise Bird." When Louise said, Hello, it was Homer Garrison on the other end. As you would expect of two close friends, they both enjoyed a laugh as Garrison recounted for her the events of his men's visit to Galveston.

Advertisement in Galveston Isle Magazine, June 1949

History

Pop Snow

Moorman Harry Snow was born in Evansville, Indiana in 1893, went through the eighth grade, moved to Galveston on November 4, 1911, entered the movie theater business on that very day, became known around here as Pop Snow, and hand wrote his five-page autobiography on June 30, 1958, at his home at 4411 Avenue N.

His daughter, Dorothy Snow Lucas, co-founder of Luke's Supermarket and Deli, sent me a copy of that autobiography. She had transcribed it by typewriter. She was careful to leave in his spelling and grammatical errors because she said that to have taken them out would have somehow ruined his story. She was right about that.

She said that in addition to his autobiography, she still has the old black pliers and screwdriver the two of them had used each year, when she was young, to put together the model railroad and Christmas scene under the Christmas tree. You see, Pop Snow and little Dorothy were buddies from the very beginning.

Pop Snow came to Galveston because his mother had married a Galveston barber, E.E. Elder, after her first husband had died. Elder's barber shop was at 21st and Mechanic St. Just eighteen, Pop Snow took a job as a doorman and relief projectionist at the Vaudette Theater, which was adjacent to the United Cigar Store at 21st and Market. Directly across the street was the Dixie No. 1 Theater, then a block to the west was the Leader Theater.

The other movie houses here at the time, he wrote, were the Majestic, Crystal No 1, Crystal Majestic, Tremont, and a small theater on the beach also known as the Crystal. The cost for an adult ticket was the same as that for a child, five cents. But most movies back then were no longer than a half-hour.

"The Queen Theater opened in 1912, and became a vaudeville theater the next year. It had a beautiful Pilcher organ and a fourteen-piece orchestra, which was directed by Mr. Fred Ward. His orchestra was quite popular in the city at that time." The Queen seated 300 people.

When Pop Snow first arrived in Galveston, the first talkie, "The Jazz Singer" hadn't been made, the theaters were cooled by ceiling fans, and the projectors had no take-up reels, so as the film ran through the projector's sprockets, it curled free-form into a big box on the projection booth floor.

Since the movies were about a half-hour in length, downtown workers frequently would have lunch, see a show, and get back to their offices, all within their hour lunch break.

Metal output and take-up cassettes for film hadn't been invented, so the projectionists also had to be astute firemen, since the silver and sulfur coated celluloid film was frequently ignited by the heat from the projector's bulb.

When film ignited, it did so with a big flash and the theater would stink to high heaven for days thereafter.

Pop Snow and his family were originally members of a somewhat less than socially tolerant fundamentalist church. The "Rosebud Club" was sponsored by the church, and the Snows enjoyed the fellowship at the meetings. But as things would have it, it wasn't long until the church members found out Pop Snow worked as a projectionist at a movie house.

"Everyone knows that's evil," the pastor told him. "Get another job, or you'll have to discontinue your membership as a Rosebud and as a member of this church!" So Pop Snow and his family joined Trinity Episcopal Church, Snow opting to remain in show business. Episcopalians saw nothing wrong with being employed in the movie industry.

Just prior to 1927, Pop Snow was president of the West End Civic Club when it led the way in securing government funding for the grade raising of the West End between 39th Street to 57th Street.

He then tried his hand at politics, running for police and fire commissioner on Owen Barker's mayoral ticket. Owen Barker was attorney Jerry Barker's father. Snow was defeated by pharmacist Frank Williamson's father, R. P. (Dick) Williamson. Pop Snow also ran for a school board position at least two times thereafter, and was defeated in those races as well.

But most old-time Galvestonians remember Pop Snow as the founder of the island's most successful baseball program. In 1939, he organized the City Baseball League, and convinced the commissioner of public streets, Raymond Steward, to build four diamonds near where Moody Gardens is today. As World War II progressed, the property was taken over by the federal government. Baseball was discontinued.

In 1950, the diamonds were moved to a full square block of Heard's Lane "through the efforts of city recreation director Bernard Davis." Irving Ducoff was the president of the League when that season opened, and Snow and Stewart received bronze plaques for their years of dedication.

While no one is quite sure why he was called Pop, with his signature white crew cut, not a single person was ever able to think of a surname that would have been more appropriate.

Pop Snow (center)

Dr. Peete and the Home He Designed to Save His Family

In those days, the poor of the city lived in small houses and shanties on the far east-end of the Island, reserving the middle part of the city for the homes of the middle-class and wealthy.

Dr. George W. Peete, whose title was Health Physician of Galveston, had moved here six years before. It was now 1875, and the city's shipping business was still inflating its chest, money was still flowing freely, and the rich were still throwing and attending one party after another.

Peete quickly became known throughout the city as a man of great character and strength. And while he was well educated, refined and loved by most, all felt that his greatest asset was that he was "the friend of the poor and the counselor to the weak."

By the time Peete and his family had moved here, the city was beating all odds, continuing to ride a wave of prosperity, even though it had been inflicted with severe damage through the hurricanes of 1818, 1837 and 1867.

Each time it had rebuilt. Each time the economy had gotten better than it was before.

Dr. Peete thought he could do his best work if he were the advisor and physician to the poor. To do that, his judgment told him, he and his family should lived near them. He selected a site at Fort Point, at the very eastern tip of the island. It was also the area where the government maintained its ship yards.

Peete knew that by building his family home there, that it would be a sitting duck for wind and water damage when the next hurricane came to the Island. Nevertheless, as the person he saw himself, he felt he must take that chance.

After much study of the construction techniques used for homes and vessels, Peete designed a home that was in two sections. The lower section would follow the conventional building parameters used for homes. The upper section, however, would be built like a raft, and it would be attached so that it would automatically detach and float if the gulf waters rose up to it.

Peete reasoned that if that were to happen, he and his family would be safe on the second floor raft, and that it would eventually float them to the city where they could be rescued.

Dr. Peete supervised the entire construction, using carpenters to build the first floor, and experienced ship building mechanics to build the second floor.

Five years later, on the 14th day of September, a hurricane which would shortly thereafter be judged as the most severe storm that had ever hit the coast, came barging its way ashore. For four days it blew things apart, floated things away, and injured and killed men, women, children and animals.

The first morning of the storm was Wednesday, and by 10 o'clock the government yards at Fort Point had been shut down, and the workers had gone into the city for refuge. By 1 o'clock, the remaining three men from the yards struck out on foot toward home. The waters by then were so high that the men soon knew they would be unable to make it, so they tried to return to Fort Point. The rising water didn't wait for them. They drowned.

Meanwhile, it was well known throughout the city that Dr. Peete and his family were still at their Ft. Point home, but it was also well known that the Peetes home was built to allow the upper story to float them to safety. No one gave serious consideration that the Peetes were in jeopardy. No one went to check.

By 4 o'clock, Dr. Peete realized that no one was coming to rescue his family. Worse yet, the upper floor had not disconnected and begun to float. Peete wondered if his building plan would work.

Dr. Peete put his wife, two of his grandchildren, the family's servant and her son in the Peete's boat, and sent them toward the city. Since there was not room for all in the boat, Dr. Peete and his eldest grandson remained behind. It was the plan that the boat would return to pick up Dr. Peete and his grandson, and take them to safety as well.

By 5 o'clock, however, there had been no sign of the

boat. Peete and his grandson, standing on the upper gallery, began signaling for help. Several attempted to reach them. All failed. Thereafter, no more boats came near.

They were now alone with the elements, their safety solely dependent upon the engineering and construction of the unusual house.

Oddly by now the winds had started to subside, blowing less than forty miles an hour, but the sea remained angry and continued to tear at the home's first floor.

As the doctor and his grandson stood on the gallery, looking toward the city, not knowing whether their family had made it to safety, the first floor gave away. Sometime during the night, although no one knows how or why, the upper floor raft that was suppose to save them from death, didn't.

On Tuesday, the bodies of Dr. George W. Peete and his grandson were found. Flags immediately went to half staff, and most of the remaining citizens of Galveston put their own problems aside, and followed the burial procession to Magnolia Cemetery which became the final resting place.

Within a couple of days, the water was calm, the winds were dry, and could only be described as gentle breezes. Thousands of oleander bushes throughout the island began to profusely bloom. Like the abusive drunk who sobers up and with his charm begs and gets forgiveness, most of the survivors of the 1875 hurricane fell again for the Island's charming personality, and decided to remain. Perhaps it wasn't so bad after all, they reasoned.

Battle of Galveston: John Magruder Was a "Give me Liberty or Give Me Death" Kind of a Guy

On Monday, October 6, 1862, the Union Navy blocked Galveston's port. On Christmas Day, Union ground troops landed and placed the entire island under Northern control.

Elsewhere, a West Point graduate named John Magruder had shown such leadership in the Mexican War, that he had been promoted to the rank of General. Now that the Mexican War was over and the Civil War was underway, he took command of New Mexico, Texas and Arizona for the Confederate War Department of Texas. He took that command four days after the Union Navy blocked Galveston's port.

General John Bankhead Magruder was one of those "give me liberty or give me death" kind of soldiers. Everything he did was fully dressed in drama. Even the custom-made uniforms loaded with gold braids and metals that he wore bore that out. He rarely spoke a sentence that was anything other than a flowery Shakespearean-esque pontification.

Once, after he had won the first land battle of the

Civil War for the Confederacy, under a flag of truce he allowed the opposing general to remove a slain officer from the battlefield. As the enemy was taking the officer's body, Magruder mounted a nearby tree stump and modulated in his best oratory style so all could hear, "We part as friends, but on the field of battle we meet as enemies!" This flair for the dramatic earned him the nickname, "Prince John."

While Magruder was stationed in San Diego, after the Mexican War, he studied for the Masonic Order, and became an Entered Apprenticed Mason. No one seems to question that he would have eventually become a Master Mason, but his "Prince John" persona got in the way of that when Magruder and the lodge's treasurer had a disagreement. That's when Magruder delivered an elaborate speech challenging the treasurer to a duel at sun-up. That forever stopped Magruder's furtherance in the Masonic Order.

As soon as General Magruder took over his Texas post for the Confederacy, he realized that the entire economy of the state would soon collapse if the Union blockades at Galveston weren't broken. He planned to launch his attack early on the morning of New Year's Day, 1863.

Magruder outfitted with guns two small steamboats—the Neptune and the Bayou City—and he had the decks surrounded with cotton bales to provide protection for the fighters. Volunteer ground troops were ordered to secretly cross at night, by way of the railroad bridge, from the mainland to Galveston. They formed a large semicircle around Kuhn's Wharf where the Union troops were garrisoned.

At 3:00 A.M., the morning of New Year's Day,

Magruder, in all of his fancy military regalia, stepped up and fired the first cannon shot which he had envisioned would denote the beginning of the Battle of Galveston. That shot startled the Union troops, who were not expecting an enemy assault.

And then, before he could do anything else, Prince John had to further advance his flair for the dramatic. He announced to his troops, "Now that I've done my duty as a private, I will go and attend to my duties as the general."

By contrast to the financially poor position in which the Confederacy had found itself, requiring that it use modified steamboats as warships, the Union had a copper-sheathed gunboat. It was under the command of Jonathan M. Wainwright, Jr., who would later be the posthumous grandfather of General Jonathan M. Wainwright, III, of World War II fame. Wainright, Jr.'s ship was named the Harriet Lane.

The Harriet Lane was successful in sinking Magruder's cotton-bale-outfitted Neptune. It was then that Magruder ordered the Bayou City to ram the Harriet Lane in such a way as to cause the two vessels to become permanently bonded together. Then the troops of the Bayou City boarded the Harriet Lane, and captured it through hand to hand combat.

Another Union ship, the Westfield, on its way to provide backup for the Harriet Lane, had run aground near Galveston. Magruder sent demands to the Union commodore who was on the Westfield that if there was to be a truce, the commodore would have to order flags of truce flown on the entire Union fleet, and surrender it within three hours.

That was when the commodore tried to destroy the Westfield rather than surrender it, and blew it and himself up in the process.

Meanwhile, Wainwright also wanted to be obstinate. He refused to surrender, and was killed by a shot to the head delivered from the gun of a Confederate soldier who was a fellow Mason.

Masonic prisoners being held by Magruder vouched to the Confederate Masons that the slain Commander Jonathan Mayhew Wainright, Jr., was not only the son of an Episcopal bishop of the Diocese of New York, but was a Mason in good standing.

The Union prisoners asked for a Masonic Burial for Wainright. The Worshipful Master of Galveston's Harmony Lodge was Philip Tucker, and he was a major on Magruder's staff.

Tucker agreed to open the Galveston lodge and hold the Masonic burial. Hearing this, Magruder said to him, "Major Tucker, I hear you intend to bury the remains of Commander Wainright tomorrow with Masonic honors. Is it true?"

Tucker said, "Yes, sir, and I hope you will give it military honors."

"Who ever heard of burying a dead enemy with Masonic and military honors?" demanded Magruder.

"General Magruder, when Lieutenant Colonel Rogers of the Second Texas fell, the Federal authorities gave the body Masonic and military burial, and it is said that you, sir, are never to be outdone in courtesy to a friend or enemy."

"Not by a sight," Magruder quickly responded, so the full Masonic and military funeral was held.

On Friday, the Harmony Lodge opened the funeral with the resolution, "that the members of this Lodge, appreciating the spirit and force of Masonic ties, will not allow their feelings and prejudice and love of righteous cause to obliterate from their hearts and minds the merciful teaching of the Order; that it does not conflict with their duties as patriotic citizens to respond to calls of mercy by a prostrate political foe, or to administer the last rite of the Order to the remains of a Mason of moral worth, although yesterday they met as an armed enemy in mortal combat in which the deceased parted with his life."

Having been established in 1840, not only was Galveston's Harmony Lodge one of the first Masonic lodges in Texas, but it was also the first and last Masonic lodge, north or south, "to conduct the Masonic burial service for a Mason killed in mortal combat as an enemy."

And as a result of General Magruder's proficiency as a military leader, Galveston stayed a part of the Confederacy for the remainder of the war, and the economy of Texas remained stable as a result.

But when it came time for the surrender of the Confederacy, General Magruder was unable to live with loss, so he joined the army of Maximilian in Mexico. When Maximilian was defeated, Magruder moved back to Texas and to Houston where he died in poverty in 1871.

Later, some of Magruder admirers, who were also citizens of Galveston, felt he should be buried on the island that he had saved. It took several years of fund raising, but finally enough money was collected to buy a funeral vault and a Galveston burial lot for General John Bankhead Magruder's final interment.

How Galveston Saved Itself from Self-Destruction in 1901

"The sea wall is completed; the grade raising is done; the bonds of the city are back at par; Galveston is back on its feet again; and the great storm is only history.

"As an emergency form of government, there can be no question that the Commission has proved to be wonderfully prompt, energetic and economical," wrote Ernest S. Bradford, Ph.D., in his 1911 book, *Commission Government in American Cities*.

Prior to 1900, like most American cities, Galveston used the aldermanic form of government. Representatives were elected from and to specifically represent each neighborhood. Thus, a city's governmental body had as many aldermen as it had neighborhoods. Consequently, there could be no division of the responsibilities with respect to the operation of the city's business. Every decision was a committee decision.

Called the Galveston Plan, the commissioner form of government was invented in 1901, as a means to save Galveston from financial ruin. Had Galveston continued under the aldermanic form, there seems to be universal agreement that bankruptcy would have been inevitable. Ironically, that had been obvious to business leaders for at least ten years prior to the 1900 Storm.

The last few years Galveston had operated under the aldermen, each year the city's income had fallen about $100,000 below its obligations. The deficit had been covered by the sale of bonds, and a prayer that somehow a miracle would cause the financial problems to resolve themselves, by themselves, the following year. That never happened.

A total of $2,850,000 in general obligation bonds had been issued. It represented more than ten percent of the assessed values of the all of the property on the island. It was then that the credit market decided that the evidence was empirical: Galveston was drowning in debt, and the aldermen had no plan for resolution. The credit market's money window for Galveston was slammed shut.

With no longer a place to get cash to cover the deficits, the city began kiting paychecks for city salaries. Two hundred thousand dollars in paychecks bounced. Then the city was forced to issue scrip to cover salaries. Like most scrip, Galveston's issue only occasionally had value, and when it did, it only had a little. City employees began resigning.

By 1900, not only was the city deeply in debt, but it now faced two other problems—if Galveston were to survive, it needed to rebuild public confidence in city government, and it needed to rebuild a city and its economy that had been all but totally destroyed by a hurricane.

George Sealy was the chairman of the Deep Water

Committee. That group decided to take the lead, and they appointed a group of three of their fellow committee members to rewrite the city charter: Col. Walter Gresham, a former member of congress and a prominent attorney; F.D. Minor, a lawyer; and R. Waverley Smith, who was president of the First National Bank of Galveston.

The committee of three studied the charters of several cities—cities that had been able to save themselves from bankruptcy.

Just twenty-five years before, Memphis had found itself within a few bucks of insolvency, the result of an epidemic of yellow fever. To the Galveston charter committee, that sounded similar to the problem Galveston had incurred as a result of the 1900 Storm. Memphis had changed its form of government from the aldermanic form to a board of governors. The result was a remarkable financial recovery.

The idea that Gresham, Minor and Smith came up with was similar. They recommended for Galveston's new governing body the replication of a publicly held corporation. All five members would be elected by the vote of all registered voters, and, other than the mayor-president, each member would have a specific area of responsibility. For an example, the commissioner of streets and public property would manage the city's physical assets. A commissioner's term would be two years.

In 1901, the committee sent its proposed new charter to the Texas legislature, and the city government of Galveston was changed in that session to that of a board of commissioners.

The governor of Texas was J.D. Sayers, and he unilaterally decided that it was up to him to appoint the first Galveston board of commissioners. That was immediately challenged, and the Texas Court of Criminal Appeals decided that it was not within the governor's authority to appoint all of the board members. A majority of them had to be elected by the qualified voters of the city of Galveston.

Galveston city attorney, Judge J.Z.H. Scott, then wrote an amendment to the new charter that provided that all commissioners and the mayor had to be elected. There was no sympathy for allowing the governor to appoint any of them.

The first slate was overwhelmingly chosen by Galvestonians: Judge William T. Austin, mayor-president; I.H. Kempner, commissioner of finance and revenue; V.E. Austin, commissioner of streets and public property; H.C. Lange, commissioner of waterworks and sewerage; and, A.P. Norman, commissioner of police and fire protection.

The commission's first order of business was to retain engineers to plan the building of a sea wall, and the raising of the grade of all of the property behind it. The second was to collect all of the past-due taxes. Kempner's analysis proved-up that that in itself would get the city solvent.

The engineers for the sea wall and grade-raising were hired, and Kempner, on behalf of the City of Galveston, enforced the collection of back taxes.

Shortly, the city was able to pay off the entire bond indebtedness, a new public confidence stepped in, and the local and national feelings were that now Galveston could achieve any goal it set before it.

All of this happened while the rest of the world watched. And, as with anything that proves to be successful, it wasn't long before other cities, some 300 in all, decided to adopt the Galveston Plan. Many of those were among the largest in America—New Orleans, Dallas, Birmingham, San Antonio, Newark, Birmingham, even Houston.

It is interesting to note that finally Galveston had taken the advice of one of its most vocal critics. Forty-five years earlier, Ferdinand Flake had written in his newspaper, "Flake's Bulletin:" "If the merchants, business men, mechanics and all others interested in the welfare of Galveston would get together . . . and nominate a ticket composed of the most prosperous, active and clear-headed citizens...those who have a reputation for probity and financial success, our city would flourish . . . and her credit as a municipal corporation would rank with the first in the land."

That's exactly what happened in 1901, and that's exactly how Galveston was able to survive and prosper into the new century.

In 1916, A New Hobby of Stamp Collecting Uncovered His Father's Secret Life

It was 1916. Walter Grover found himself fascinated with the prospects of a new hobby, collecting stamps. The book he found at the library, "Collecting Stamps for Fun and Profit," said that the best way to begin was to find old letters that were stored in the family's attic, basement and closets, and scavenge stamps from them.

Grover went into the attic of his family's house on Winnie St., and there he slowly uncovered a treasure. It was a treasure he would later tell friends he was sure would have soon been destroyed had he not found it when he did.

It wasn't that the stamps on those envelopes were unusual. It was the letters inside that chronicled his father's adventures that were priceless. They were stories his father had never told him.

Walter Grover knew his father, George, as the reserved, co-owner of a successful grocery and mercantile business at the corner of 22nd and Strand. The letters Walter found, though, told another story; a story of his father's exciting past-life.

Galveston Memories

Early in 1841, George Grover organized a group of Austin merchants for a political march to Santa Fe. They wanted to establish a new trade route. They made one mistake in their planning. No one who went along in Grover's group was sufficiently fluent in Spanish.

The Mexicans who caught up with the group prior to their arrival in Santa Fe, assumed they were coming to attempt a raid. Because of their limited Spanish vocabulary, Grover's group was unable to convince the Mexicans otherwise.

The heavily armed and man-powered Mexicans took the group prisoner, and marched them on foot to Mexico City where Grover and his allies were tried, convicted and jailed.

While in prison, under what he described as horrible and inhumane conditions, Grover published a newspaper which he wrote with pen and ink. It was called "The True Blue." He used the pseudonym, Simon Pure. These newspapers would later become invaluable resource documents for writers of the history of the southwest.

In 1843, Grover planned and executed a convoluted but successful escape from the Mexican prison, and made his way back to his hometown of Cincinnati. Within the year, he decided it was time for him to grow up and settle down. He began that new chapter in his life by marrying his lifelong sweetheart, Hepzy Andrews. Before the year was up, she died. There now was nothing to keep Grover in Cincinnati, so he decided to resume his prior maverick lifestyle.

He convinced Hepzy's brother to join him, and they

headed for the mystique offered by New Orleans. Shortly after they arrived in the Crescent City, they decided it was not what they had imagined, so from there they went to Panama, then traveled to the Barbary Coast. There they tried gold prospecting, but they remained restless.

Grover and Andrews heard of the fortunes that could be made in a new city called Galveston. So in 1850, they came here to invest their savings in the founding of a grocery and mercantile business. Two years later, Grover married a Galveston debutante, Eliza Ann Crane.

At 1520 Market Street, he built the home of her dreams. It remains there today. It was described by writers of the time as "the Greek Revival showplace of the century." It was there that their six children were born and raised. It was there that many of the grand social parties of the day were held.

By 1862, Grover and Andrews' business was a huge success; Grover had entered politics; he was the mayor pro-tem of the city of Galveston; and Federal gunboats had blocked the port, shelled the city, and captured it.

Since Grover had a deformed left hand, it made him unable to be a member of the Confederate military. Nevertheless, at his wife's insistence, and in his position as the city's mayor pro-tem, he went to the federal troops' headquarters in the Henley Building at 20th and Strand, to begin negotiating on behalf of the besieged city of Galveston.

As he rode by horseback from his home to the Union headquarters, the city was under fire. Grover's wife and six children remained behind in the Market Street home. His wife stood in the house's cupola and watched the shell fire around them. A number of those shells landed in their yard. At least one cannon ball penetrated the house's upstairs south wall.

Throughout the years thereafter, Walter Grover and his friends would dig around in the house's yard for bullets. They would melt them down and use them to make sinkers for fishing lines and cast nets.

In another series of George Grover's letter, Walter uncovered tales of a man named Mordello. He had been one of Jean Lafitte's men. Mordello had told George Grover that Lafitte had a mistress whose first name was Theodosa. Mordello was sure that Theodosa was Theodosa Burr, the daughter of Virginia governor, Aaron Burr. She had mysteriously disappeared while on a voyage for a European holiday that her father had given her.

George Grover sold the Market Street home in early 1900, and the family moved to 1516 Winnie. A couple of months later, in the Winnie house, the family rode out the 1900 Storm. All survived. The following day, Walter Grover joined the remaining Galveston men survivors as they began sending out to sea, by barge, the bodies of those whose luck had run out the day before.

Within what seemed like mere moments, the waves started washing those very same bodies back ashore. Walter and the others dug long trenches so the corpses could be thrown in and buried. "This time the waves would not be able to sing those bodies' requiem," one newspaper eloquently said.

When he was about eighty, Walter Grover told a story of his own.

Before the grade raising that began after the 1900 Storm, there were many bayous in the city, especially in the area bound by what we now call Avenues M and N1/2 on the north and south, and 23rd and 28th Streets on the east and west. Broadway had been built high. The property to the south of it remained at sea-level grade. Broadway, therefore, was thought to serve a second purpose. It was somewhat of a levy; the city's first seawall.

To the south of Broadway, where the Moody House is today, there had been a baseball field. It had been graded under. The Beach Hotel was just to its east. In 1886, a storm caused a good deal of the property in that area to wash out. People called it the "overflow."

A day or so after the overflow, Walter walked to the beach to survey the damage. In deep holes created by the overflow where the baseball field had been, he found the remnants of a wrecked ship.

Walter worked for John Adriance & Sons. They insured boats, so he knew a lot about them. The boat parts he found in the holes were of a type and kind he had never seen before. Walter wondered what kind of boat had ship wrecked there.

In 1925, Grover was in Plymouth, Massachusetts, and it was there that he saw one of the boats that had brought the Pilgrims to America. Its name was the Sparrowhead. There Walter found the answer to his question.

Walter Grover

Galveston

If you've lived here for any length of time, you have probably heard any number of opinions as to how this once vibrant community started and then with only sixty years under its belt, fell into an economic decline that has continued for the most part since 1902.

It is somewhat paradoxical that in 1836, Michel B. Menard, a Canadian fur trader, purchased the then inhabitable part of this island from the Austin Colony for $50,000, and one hundred sixty years later the Chamber of Commerce paid almost that much to J.L. Taylor, Jr., yet another consultant in a string of many, to tell them what Galveston needs to do to reverse that ninety-six year downward trend.

There are several items from our history where the blame is usually placed to rest for the Island's fate. They are the 1900 Storm, the closing down of the illegal gambling and prostitution, and the opening of the waterway from the Gulf of Mexico to a man-made ship channel in Houston. And then old families, mainly the Moodys, the Kempners and the Sealys, get the blame for Galveston never returning to that economic prosperity. Balderdash, I say!

It's time to set history straight.

The foundation for the original economy of Galveston was the packing, storing and exporting of cotton. In fact in 1899, Galveston exported almost seventy percent of the nation's cotton, and an enormous portion of that had been grown right here on Texas soil.

In those days the basis for Texas' economy was farming cotton. It wasn't oil or rice or mercantile commerce. It was cotton farming.

In a matter of less than sixty-four years, cotton grown in Texas had made Galveston one of the richest cities in the United States, and certainly the richest in this state. But then the 1900 Storm came on September 8, and within twenty-four hours, Galveston's population had been reduced by six thousand, ten thousand more were left homeless, and all of the schools, twenty-one of the churches, and the two bridges connecting the island to the mainland were nothing but piles of wood.

Within weeks, with the help of outsiders from throughout the nation, and although people were sleeping in tents on the beach, under tar paper roofs on decapitated houses, and still surrounded by debris and the stench of death, commerce returned full steam and hope returned with it. The 1900 Storm did little to hurt the Galveston economy.

Now here's the important part, and it is, for some reason, what is usually left out of the story. The heavy rains of the 1900 Storm had spread throughout Texas, and the soil had become the most perfect environment for raising cotton anyone could remember. So by the end of 1901, almost every acre of previously unfarmed land throughout Texas had joined up with those used for cotton farming, and that land was planted with cotton.

Signs of prosperity were everywhere. Merchants were throwing credit at anyone and everyone. Galveston was again on a roll.

But then as fast as it came, it went. By June 15, 1901, the cotton throughout Texas started to turn brown. The bolls and the leaves fell to the ground, and a few days later, all of the cotton fields looked as though they had been the victim of a massive forest fire.

Here's what had happened. The 1900 Storm had passed over the Yucatan Peninsula and the edge of Mexico, and caught the newly hatched boll weevils and sent them to Texas for the very first time. They ate the crops. Galveston was broke again.

It was the last time King Cotton would ever be truly king. The rest of Texas recognized that and began to look for other ways to make a buck, and most of those ways didn't involve Galveston.

Galveston business people realized that the city had to diversify its economy rather than keep all of its eggs in that one empty basket, so the path of least resistance was to develop the tourist industry.

For that to be successful was fairly easy. Traveling great distances by car was all but impossible, so people were limited in the distance they could travel for vacations. Trains already served Galveston bringing freight to and from the port, so adding passenger cars was simple and provided additional revenues for the railroad.

Air conditioning hadn't been invented by Carrier yet, and everyone wanted to be cool in the summer. Galveston offered that solution with its gulf breezes. The beach front hotels didn't even need to keep up with maintenance as long as those breezes blew through the guest rooms, and for the most part the innkeepers did just that.

So Galveston, it seemed, could easily become the Playground of the Southwest, and with some good marketing, it did.

But as things would have it, Galveston again made no effort to prepare for its inevitable future. Air conditioning started making its way into people's homes; super highways made access to far off places easy; and air travel was no longer mainly restricted to the military. People could stay home and be cool, and for their vacations they could now travel to places where it really was cool.

Rather than build better hotels, hire even more famous headliners for the casino showrooms, and provide better attractions, Galveston tourist-business owners did just the opposite; they cut back.

Las Vegas, on the other hand, took a different tact. It hired those who had learned the hospitality trade in Galveston, and brought them there to build a Galveston on the desert. No amount of money was spared. No good idea left undeveloped. Las Vegas took the place of Galveston, and it did it without a beach, gulf waters and cool breezes.

Meanwhile in 1957, the then mayor, George Roy Clough, Texas Attorney Will Wilson and other do gooders chose to rid Galveston of gambling and prostitution. But that was all after the fact. They could have left well enough alone, and within a year or so it would have closed down by itself. It had had to struggle to last as long as it did.

What seems to always be lost in the equation is the indisputable fact that nature didn't mean for barrier islands to be industrial centers, and therefore the economics that work inland are simply not applicable to barrier islands.

The likelihood that industry of any measurable consequence will ever be enough to be a basis for Galveston's economy is remote. That has been proven time and time again over the past 100 years, even though Taylor's study insists otherwise.

Galveston is not meant to be an industrial center. It is meant to be a tropical paradise for people to live on and enjoy.

In 1889, A. Martini Was a Poor Immigrant. In 1937, He Was the Wealthiest Italian in Texas

On Thursday evening, May 27, 1937, Galveston mayor Adrian Levy stood behind a dais at the corner of 21st and Church. To the casual bystander, the occasion appeared to be a celebration of the grand opening of the most modern and well-equipped motion-picture theater in the south.

Those who were privy to the list of dignitaries—some 125 in all—saw a crowd of top theater people from New York, Hollywood, Chicago, New Mexico and Texas. To those in the know, it was obvious that the opening of the new theater was secondary to what this occasion was really all about. It was primarily to be a celebration of the life and unbelievable accomplishments of the new theater's owner, Attilleo Martini.

The man for whom the new movie theater was named was, on that very night, at seventy years old, one of the wealthiest Italian immigrants in the United States, and arguably the wealthiest in Texas. Less than fifty years before, having just arrived in America with empty pockets and little knowledge of the English language, he was a dockhand on the New York waterfront.

Martini was born in 1867 in Santa Maria del Giudice, in the province of Lucca, Italy. By sixteen, he was running a construction crew; by eighteen he was an entrepreneur on the island of Sardinia, off the African coast. At twenty-two, he married, and two months later left his new bride behind as he sailed to America to look for new opportunities for them.

His first job in New York was on the waterfront. Then he was a hotel porter. In 1890, with the money he had saved since his arrival in America, he boarded a ship and sailed to Galveston for the enormous chances of success he had heard were here for recent immigrants.

When he got to the island, he took a job as a yard laborer for the Santa Fe railroad. Within a few months, against all odds, he had raised enough capital to open a small grocery store. Soon after he added a bar and then he opened a second store. Attilleo Martini was now a success. It was then that he went back to Italy to bring his bride back with him to America. It had been just shy of five years since he had last seen her.

In 1910, at forty-three, Martini leased a building in the 2100 block of Market, and opened his first theater, the Dixie No. 1. Two years later, he built the Dixie No. 2 in the 2600 block of Market.

Just before he opened his third theater, the Crystal, he added a full orchestra in his movie houses. No one had done that before. Then he built the Key, and then in 1924 he bought the 1894 Grand Opera House and renamed it the "Martini Theater."

And it was Attilleo Martini who gave Galvestonians

their first glimpse at a picture that had a sound track. And it was Attilleo Martini whose theater showed the first outdoor talkie ever, "In Old Arizona." That was in 1929, and it was the picture that, at the last minute, actor Warner Baxter was substituted for Raoul Walsh, as the film's lead. That bit of fate allowed Baxter to earn that year's Academy award for Best Actor.

On this particular Thursday evening, another of Mayor Levy's duties was to officiate over the changing of the name of the old 1894 Grand Opera House from the "Martini Theater" to the "State Theater," so that the new theater could thereafter be the "Martini Theater." After opening remarks and speeches from the dignitaries, Levy pulled the switch that lighted the sign on the new theater at the corner of 21st and Church streets. The theater was never dark again for thirty-eight years.

Noted theatrical architect, Scott Dunne, had designed the new theater. It was built out of hollow tile and steel, and, at its highest point, it was three stories tall. Its entrance was in ducoed baked enamel in three shades of maroon. Shades of orange and yellow were used for accents.

Two years before, Martini had pooled his Galveston theater interests with those of an old friend, Karl Hoblinzelle. Hoblinzelle was another Texas motion-theater magnet. Their new joint venture was called Interstate Theaters, and by the time the new Martini opened, Interstate was operating almost every movie house in Texas.

Within time, the Interstate Theater chain was ruled a monopoly, and ordered to split up. In 1951, the Martini family's original theaters reverted to them. The State, Broadway and Oleander Drive-in remained with Interstate.

Martini's daughter, Anita, known to Galvestonians as "Big Granny," and her son, Giosue "Sonny" Martini operated the Martini after Attilleo's death in 1943, until Sonny died unexpectedly in 1968 at fifty-four.

Big Granny had her own chain of Galveston theaters: the Booker, the Carver, and the Dixie No. 3. Sonny owned the Isle.

Sonny's wife, Catherine, kept the Martini Theater open until 1970, when she leased it to the Interstate chain. It closed for good in 1975. Big Granny died in 1979. After the Martini closed, Catherine Martini moved to Las Vegas.

Other than a new roof, nothing has been done to preserve the exterior of the Martini Theater. However, inside, if the house lights were low, it would be hard to tell that within the hour, the first run of the day's feature would not be beginning. The rows of seats, the generators, projectors, and the screen are just as they were when the last show played. Only the carpet shows the decay caused it by the once leaky roof, and the concession stand, incongruously, is without popcorn.

In recent years, Giosue "Sonny" Martini's younger son, Michael, purchased from his relatives their minor interests in the Martini Theater property. Michael's hopes are someday to renovate the house and resume operations. In the meantime, he continues as the service manager for Star Motors, one of the Mercedes dealers in Houston, and as an investor in various oil interests.

Sonny's older son, Eugene Martini, also known as "Sonny," is in the seafood restaurant business. He buys freshly caught gulf shrimp and oysters and prepares them the way those of us over fifty-five remember from our childhood. It's a combination that's difficult to find in many of the other island seafood restaurants.

Giosue's older daughter, Anita Martini, who was named after Big Granny, was a Houston sports announcer. It was on April 21, 1976, that she made history by becoming the first woman to ever broadcast a major league game. It was the Houston Astros against the Cincinnati Reds. As her father did, Anita died at 54. Because of her accomplishments, the Houston Area Women's Center was dedicated to her and four other Houston women, Oveta Culp Hobby, Dominique de MenU, Angela V. Morales and Christina V. Daniels Adair.

And finally, there's Cathy Martini, the youngest daughter, named after her mother, who has been a drill-team instructor for more than twenty years. Her Klein Oaks High School team has brought in numerous national awards.

There is one more complexity of this tale: Other than Attilleo Martini and Big Granny, all of the other Martinis mentioned in this story should have had the surname, "Martinelli," not "Martini." You see Big Granny had her children by her first husband, a man named Martinelli. She divorced him, and later married her first cousin. His last name was Martini. Her children took the surname of their stepfather.

Son of Spanish Nobleman, Designed Studio Lounge and Balinese Room

Virgil Quadri grew up in the Villa Arcolaio, built in Rome by Michelangelo 500 years before. Quadri's father was the Marquis Quadrios, a Spanish nobleman. His mother was the daughter of a wealthy Cincinnati, Ohio banker named Gilmore.

The Gilmores had a villa in Florence, and it was during one of those trips to Europe that the Marquis Quadrios, thirty-eight, and Geneva Gilmore, eighteen, met while both families were on mountain climbing holidays in the Tyrolean Alps. Shortly thereafter Quadrois and Gilmore married.

Quadri attended Colegio Internacional Toriono and the University of Bologna. He moved to the U.S. in 1919, and at his mother's insistence, enrolled at M.I.T. in Cambridge, Massachusetts. He got a degree in mechanical engineering, a course of study he later claimed he hated.

"That was the biggest mistake of my life," he told Nathalie Moskowitz in 1949. "I felt I was on the wrong tract. After two years at M.I.T. there was nothing I hated more than mechanical engineering. It was just like being a bookkeeper."

"I liked art, but because I had rebuilt a bicycle as a youngster, Mother took that as a sign that my talent and life's work should be that of an engineer," he added.

Quadri's true interest was to be a working artist. In fact, while at M.I.T. he was art editor of Voo Doo, the campus magazine. In 1926, rather than pursue a career in mechanical engineering, much to his mother's dismay, he moved to New York's Greenwich Village, and set up shop as a fill-fledged painter.

Several years later, Quadri learned that the famous Marshall Field's family was looking for an interior designer for its Chicago store as well as for the fine home of its president. He applied for the job and got it. From that came jobs to decorate other fine homes in Lake Forest, Illinois and an elaborate Masonic Temple in Freeport.

From the notoriety he got from those commissions, he was retained to decorate the Parisian Bar of the Hollander Hotel in Cleveland, the Century Room of the Adolphus Hotel in Dallas, and the Balinese Room of the Hotel Claridge in Memphis. Sketches and photographs of his work were reproduced in Architectural Forum magazine.

Meanwhile, Sam and Rose Maceo were operating a Chinese restaurant, the Sui Jen, on a 300-foot pier they had built in 1922, and that stretched over the Gulf of Mexico from 21st Street. The Sui Jen's chef had been the personal cook for Gen. John Pershing during World War I. His name was Go-Bo.

Go-Bo died in the late 1930s, and when friends were going through his belongings, they found more than 100-gallon jars of rice in his room that they later learned he had taken from the Sui Jen, a cup or two at a time.

Following Chinese tradition, he had accumulated his stash of rice to nourish himself on his trip to the "celestial unknown."

With the death of Go-Bo, in 1941 Sam and Rose Maceo decided to change the Chinese decor and the menu of the Sui Jen. They also decided that the new supper club would be the gem of their future Galveston operations, and that the Hollywood Dinner Club would be closed for good.

It was then that Sam Maceo scouted the United States for its best interior designer, and then that he discovered the work of Quadri.

It was Quadri who suggested the new name of the club be the "Balinese Room." His designs included huge murals and life-sized glass palm trees. Colored glass water floats, waxed mangos, bananas and grapes hung from the ceiling. The bamboo furniture, the carpet and the lighting all added to the feeling, you were outside near the shore's edge.

In addition to his skills as an artist and conventional decorator, Quadri was a lighting expert. In the late 40s, the Maceos brought him back to make the Balinese Room even more beautiful. That time he installed a special system that automatically dimmed the dining room lights as the evening waned. In the concave ceiling, he recessed a multitude of mini-lights that resembled starlight.

The Balinese Room never closed a night during this renovation period. Each morning at 3 a.m. the workmen would begin where they had left off the previous afternoon. By 5 p.m. they would have the room painted and cleaned up, and ready for the evening's business, only to tear a part of it out the following morning.

The Balinese Room became engulfed in flames on October 3, 1954. The probable cause of the fire was faulty electrical wiring. When it went up in flames, so did the entire wardrobe of singer-entertainer Sophie Tucker, who was to open the following week. And Quadri's work went with it.

The building that housed the Turf Grill, Studio Lounge and Western Room, where the Bank of America's Galveston's main branch is today, burned in the late 40s, and Quadri was called back in 1949 to decorate the new Studio Lounge.

"The best thing in the whole room is the lighting," Quadri said after he had completed the job. "I designed a twisted cone that stops the light but still gives even distribution. Over ninety-eight percent of the light source in the room comes from black light and neon made especially for this commission by the Lighting Institute of Chicago."

The walls were crimson and green tufted panels. Heavy white baroque frames surrounded the surrealistic murals that were above every banquette. The chairs at the dining tables were covered in a zebra-striped material. The bathroom fixtures were maroon.

After completing his Studio Lounge commission,

Quadri returned to Chicago where he built a large, luxury apartment house at 60 Bellevue Place, but he kept his small cabin on the beach in Galveston.

When the Balinese Room was rebuilt after the 1954 fire, Quadri was legally blind, but with the help of other artists to do his painting, the Balinese Room was replicated to its original splendor.

But then Hurricane Carla hit in 1961, and once again the famous building sustained major damage. It was put back together by 1963. The Maceo family sold it in 1967. By then the Studio Lounge, Turf Grill and the Western Room had closed as well. On its site was being built the First Hutchings-Sealy National Bank building.

None of the work Virgil Quadri did in Galveston remains and the memory of it is dying as well.

Balinese Room Scenes

Hurricanes

The Surprise Ending to a Carriage Ride

While there are very few left on this earth who can recall the hurricane that by the Sunday morning of September 9, 1900, had left Galveston Island with 32,000 survivors, 6,000 injured, 5,000 dead and 10,000 homeless, nevertheless, new stories by those who survived are still being found and recounted, and those told before continue being spun again and again.

My favorite concerns two men, at the time in their eighties, who had grown up on the Island, but had only become friends as adults. The friendship has prospered, and for more than fifty years, they and their families had spent a lot of time together. One was a well-known doctor and the other a prominent businessman.

The two men were Rotarians, and always sat together at the same table back in the days when the club met at the old Galvez Hotel. And as the elderly often do, they frequently reminisced between them about days gone by, entertaining themselves, as well as the other six much younger men at their table, with their stories.

On this particular Wednesday at the Rotary meeting, during lunch the subject between the doctor and the businessman was the 1900 Storm. The businessman said that he and his brother, at the time both of grammar school age, had noticed the weather was acting strange on Saturday, September 8, and they decided to walk from their family's home near Broadway up 23rd Street to Beach to see what the gulf was doing.

There was a local weather service in those days headed by Dr. I.M. Cline, and Cline had noticed the barametric pressure had dropped to 29.55 inches and the tide had risen four feet. He hitched up his carriage and raced up and down the beach telling everyone that he felt a dangerous hurricane was on its way, and all must evacuate their homes and either leave the island or move to strong and tall downtown buildings.

By contrast to Cline's analysis, although the wind was picking up and the tide had risen, the sun was shining and nothing appeared alarming to the boys. However after hearing Dr. Cline's warning, they decided they'd better get back home.

Since there was no seawall then, the businessman told his friend, the doctor, that as he and his brother walked toward home, the water rose on 23rd Street to almost waist deep, and it was accompanied by an increasing under current and a much stronger wind. The sun went away, and the skies changed from clear and sunny to dark and ominously cloudy.

The boys still had quite away to go before they would reach home, and they became concerned that they might drown before they could get there.

About that time, the businessman said, a horse drawn carriage came along side of them. There was a family inside, but the driver told the boys to hop on top of the luggage carrier on the back of the carriage, and he would take them along with the family inside to the Tremont Hotel near 23rd and Church. Even though they wanted to go to their home, the young boys did what they were told.

As soon as the carriage arrived at the hotel, the water had risen even higher and the winds had become even stronger. Rain was now pouring down. It was obviously imperative that the family inside of the carriage, as well as the boys who had ridden on the outside luggage carrier, get inside and to one of the upper floors if they were to survive.

The hotel was packed with others who were also seeking safety.

As the businessman wove his tale for his friend, the doctor, and the other six now wide-eyed men at the table, the doctor's face started becoming pale, and tears began running down his face, but he didn't say a word until the businessman had finished the entire story.

Then the doctor said in an almost inaudible whisper, "That was my family and me who were inside that carriage. I've always wondered who the boys were who hitched the ride. Never hearing anything further from them or about them after we arrived at the Tremont Hotel, I thought they had been among the casualties of the Great Storm."

With that, the two men embraced and at that

moment their already strong friendship became even stronger, while all of the others at the table began to cheer and clap.

Mother and children in peril from the flood. Artist unknown.

Hurricane Carla: Event That Marked the Island's New Beginning

It was Monday morning, September 11, 1961. Jack Bushong was the thirty-three-year-old manager of the Hotel Galvez. Labor Day had passed, marking the end of the tourist season, yet, oddly, every room in the hotel had been sold since the preceding Friday.

Jack Bushong

For the first time in as long as anyone could remember, Galvestonians feared a hurricane. This one was named Carla, and the predictions were that if it squarely hit the island, there would be an enormous amount of property damage, and there could be many lives lost from a storm surge that would most assuredly ascend from the island's bay side.

For those who could afford it, leaving home and going to the highest point on the island, the seawall, and riding out Carla in one of the beach front hotels seemed to be the safest decision. Old time Galveston families did not accept the idea of evacuation from the island. My family was one of those, and it remains an unwritten contract that we keep with our birthplace.

About ten that morning, from one of our third story Galvez suite windows, I watched the companion pier to the east of the Balinese Room, the Dreamland Cafe, blow apart—some pieces flew toward the seawall, others landed in the waters below. Giant waves were following the arc design of the seawall, flying at least thirty feet into the air before the strongest parts of them crashed on the street, then ran toward the bay.

Next the platform that was the floor of the joint kitchen of the Dreamland and the Balinese Room became fully exposed, then it canted toward the east as pilings underneath broke away. Within moments thereafter, the last piece of kitchen equipment, an enormous range, slid down the platform and drowned in the gulf. So much for the Dreamland.

I knew then and at that moment of that day, the event signified the Galveston persona that I knew and loved would soon be no more. Today I am sure that analysis was accurate.

Those who were not born here before September 11, 1961, and who were not fully cognitive then, as far as I'm concerned, can only call themselves "boi's." They are not "BOI's" because they never saw and experienced, and therefore can't have loved, the *real* Galveston. Those who were born elsewhere, but lived here and experienced that past era can accurately call themselves BOI's.

On the following Wednesday, our family began our trip home. Along the way we saw the path that a tornado had begun at the seawall's edge on 23rd Street, destroying building after building as it cut its new roadway to the downtown.

The Buccaneer Hotel was so severely damaged that it would never open its doors as a hotel again. The entire middle section of Murdoch's was gone. Frankie Laine, Phil Harris and others had performed on that porch just a few years before. Each time thousands of visitors had crowded the street below for the free show.

Gaido's had been founded on Murdoch's. Many teenagers had danced weekends at the Blue Room, a nightclub run by teachers and counselors from our public schools. The places of those memories were now so much splintered lumber in the waters below.

The Pleasure Pier at 25th, whose building had survived nearly twenty-five years of prior storms, was ripped open like a can of cheap tuna fish. I wished for the best, but it wasn't hard to conclude that no one would ever again dance in its Marine Ballroom. No more water shows at the pier's end. Probably no more Pleasure Pier.

The car radio said that the tornado had done major damage to the Galveston Orphans Home, the courthouse, St. Mary's School, the City Auditorium and Ursuline Convent. It had wiped out warehouses, businesses and home after home. It had killed and injured people as well—some prominent people, some just average Joes.

And this tornado was an anomaly. It had rotated clockwise rather than counter-clockwise; it had a width of about 350 feet; and it walked through a couple of miles of the island before it went back into the sky from where it had come. We had been taught in school that tornadoes never struck islands.

In what seemed to have been only moments before Carla's arrival, Galveston had decided to no longer hold its famous Splash Day, an annual first weekend in May celebration that officially marked the beginning of the tourist season. It had been stopped the moment the college visitors had become unruly. They had tried to mock the script of the Connie Francis movie of the year before, "Where the Boys Are." Galveston officials would not give Splash Day a second chance.

The previous year, the commission form of government that had ruled the island for almost sixty years had been voted out, and what was judged to be a government that would be not only efficient, but would prevent corruption had taken its place.

That marked the end of mayoral campaigns for strong civic leaders like Adrian Levy, Brantly Harris, Henry Flagg, George Fraser, Herbert Y. Cartwright and George Roy Clough

In 1957, the things that would make Las Vegas strong and wealthy had been transferred from here, where they had been since 1922, to there. Most business leaders said they were glad to see them go.

The final group of important entrepreneurs of Galveston, the ones who had made the majority of their wealth from island ventures, had or would soon pass on. Sam Maceo died in 1951; Rose Maceo and W. L. Moody, Jr. in 1954; George Sealy in 1945; Dan Kempner in 1956, and his brother, I. H. Kempner, at 94, in 1967; C. P. Evans in 1962; W. A. Kelso in 1964

By 1963, Christie "the Beachcomber" Mitchell, Galveston's best known promoter and public relations person, had to revert to writing more about "old times" than "present times," because there were no more glamorous present times.

Stars had stopped coming to Galveston. Those who had been brought in by promoter Norman Clark to perform at the City Auditorium no longer came because the auditorium had been destroyed by Carla's partner in crime, the tornado. The only forum that remained was the Moody Center, and entertainers and audiences knew it to be an inappropriate venue.

Even Gorgeous George and the other wrestlers who, for years, had filled the City Auditorium week after week, couldn't do it at the Moody Center.

The beautiful and glamorous beach front night clubs closed one by one. The Maceos' amusement park at 23rd and Seawall didn't reopen one summer. The famous Derby merry-go-round at 25th was dismantled and never reassembled. Its valuable hand-carved wooden horses were stored in the Hollywood Club to gather dust and the neglect cobwebs mark. The Mountain Speedway roller coaster missed opening for the first time one summer.

Only the Jack Tar Hotel, across from Stewart Beach, kept up its front—beautiful rooms in a beautiful setting, wonderful restaurants, a fine private night club with nightly entertainment—that is until its longtime manager, Ed Leach, retired and the company sold the property to those who didn't have that same sense of pride.

A group of business people decided that if a couple of blocks of Postoffice Street were to be made a pedestrian park, and automobile parking moved to lots, the retail stores that fronted it would get a new life. Instead we said bye-bye to Plantowsky's, E. S. Levy's, Nathan's, J. Lewis Lopez, J. C. Penny's, Woolworth's, Grant's, Galveston Piano Company, Zales and Sam J. Williams'. Eiband's survived a while longer.

And the movie houses, and many of our famous restaurants went out of business. No more Martini Theater, no more Manuel's stuffed flounder. Even the downtown shoe repair shops and barber shops closed one by one.

Stores, banking houses and businesses previously owned by locals were replaced by those owned by major corporations. Houston came closer, and with Houston came more shopping choices. Galvestonians fell to the temptation.

What had made Galveston unique had been taken away as a result of the advancement of a false premises, that Galveston could only progress if it conformed. If you think about it, that was an odd conclusion, since the reason Galveston had succeeded for the previous 150 years was because it had chosen to be different.

Religion

Recounting His First Memory of His Life on Earth

He told me that his very first memory as a human began at approximately 10:45 on the morning of April 23, 1943. It was a Sunday. Two months thereafter, almost to the day, he would celebrate only his third birthday.

And now, fifty-five years later, he remembers the whole scene. He said he was dressed in blue cotton duck short pants, a starched white long sleeved dress shirt, and a navy blue clip-on bow tie that had ponies printed on it. He had on Buster Brown white high top leather shoes.

Some years later, his mother had told him that she was sure the entire outfit had come from Robert I. Cohen's, a department store that was on the corner of 22nd and Market, and that her mother, here from Louisiana to visit, had taken him downtown by city bus to buy his new outfit.

She also had told him he had gotten his first barbershop haircut on the Saturday before, at a one-man shop near 43rd and Avenue S. She thought the barber's name was Paul Wasshauer. The boy's daddy had told her, when the two had gotten home, that all had gone well until Wasshauer stropped the straight razor and started to give the haircut its finishing touches, a straight line on each of their son's cheeks to terminate his sideburns. At that point the boy had given up being brave and cried.

On this Sunday, though, his freshly cut dark brown hair, parted on the left, was plastered tight against his head with Vaseline petroleum jelly because hair tonic wasn't available to civilians during the war years.

He was standing on the lawn of Galveston's Trinity Episcopal Church in his new outfit, holding a bouquet of flowers from his mother's flower bed. The whole family, grandma included, had driven to the church in his dad's 1940 black Oldsmobile, a car, he said, that would still be taking them to church until the 1950 Fords came out.

I asked him how he knew the exact month and day of the year of that Sunday on the lawn at Trinity, and he said he had looked it up a couple of years ago. He said it was easy to find on a perpetual calendar since he knew that particular Sunday had been Easter.

"I can take you to the church now, and show you within less than a three-square-foot margin of error, where I was standing, and I know that I was facing what I call 'Galveston east.'

"On that late Easter morning, the oak trees were still glistened from an early morning dew, and they were giving off that pungent sour odor that only oaks have. A family of squirrels was playing around and up and down one of them, mindless that more than a hundred children were nearby.

"The plush new light-green spring growth of the St. Augustine grass had been groomed by the sexton, and there were scores of white lilies in the church's flower beds. Bees were darting in and out of the centers of them.

"The sun was bright and was reflecting off of the Ball High School dome across the street. The temperature was probably in the mid 60s, and the sky was perfectly clear.

"I can bring the entire picture into my mind at a moment's notice," he reconfirmed.

Gathered with him on the lawn of the church was almost every child, even to college age, who was registered in the church's Sunday School. Like him, many had hands full of flowers they had brought from their home flower beds. Others were holding in front of them flag poles with square banners made of white silk attached. Embroidered on each banner were the words, "He Is Risen!" One of the older boys held a large cross. Another held the shepherd's staff which would precede the bishop in the procession.

"Because there was no air conditioning in the church building then, the enormous stained glass windows were folded out for ventilation, and at precisely 11 o'clock, Trinity's minister, the Rev. Edmund H. Gibson, prayed aloud at the back of the church, 'May the words of our mouths and the meditations of our hearts be always acceptable in thy site, O Lord, our strength and redeemer.'

"Then all ranks of the big Henry Pilcher's Sons pipe organ began to sound out the glorious 18th-century hymn, '*Lyra Davidica.*' Thomas G. Rice, the church's organist, who was also a reporter for the "Galveston Daily News," soloed a stanza before the choir and congregation began to sing.

"Inside, the church was filled with parents, grandparents and friends—several hundred all-told—and after the organ introduction, everyone began to sing in unison, 'Jesus Christ is risen today, Alleluia! Our triumphant holy day, Alleluia! Who died once upon the cross, Alleluia! suffer to redeem our loss. Alleluia!'

"As they sang," he went on, "we children lined up and marched, preceding the bishop, in unison from the garth into the old gothic church building, and up the middle aisle. When we reached the steps to the altar, each of us who was carrying flowers sunk the stems of our bouquet into one of the holes in a big white wooden cross. Then we lined up in multiple rows and faced the congregation, the cross of flowers behind us. Those with banners were at the right and left ends of those, like me, who had brought bouquets.

"'. . .unto Christ our heavenly King. Alleluia! Who endured the cross and grave . . .' the several hundred voices comprising the choir and congregation continued, trying unsuccessfully to overcome the power of the hundreds of sounding organ pipes, the stops fully opened, the bellows providing maximum pressure on them.

"But all of a sudden I noticed that one voice was now resonating above the organ, the choir, and the other congregants. It was an enormously strong operatic voice, and it refused to be drowned out. It had taken the lead.

"I'll never forget the glorious sound. I was to later

Trinity Church, April 23, 1943

learn that it was that of Galveston's Dorothy Dow, who four years later, at twenty-six, would make her operatic debut with the Philadelphia Symphony under the direction of the famous maestro, Eugene Ormandy. Shortly after her debut, by the way, she became the leading soprano of La Scala, Milan. Her dad was the Chevrolet dealer here in those days.

"As the result of the sum total of all of those things that contributed to that Easter Sunday in my life, fifty-five years later I remember that day in such finite detail," he concluded, "and I remember not one thing in my life before that day.

"On that occasion I became tied, for a lifetime, to the importance of God, family and friends, music, church, plus the beauty of a Galveston springtime, and the serenity of life as it is on this wonderful island."

As I have pondered this tale in recent months, I have wondered how many parents seize a similar opportunity to give their own children their first memory of life.

School Prayer: Prior to 1963 Prayer Brought Educators a Different Challenge

McKee Andrus recently died. H. Rudolph "Pop" Smart died a few years before him. In both cases, there were several letters to the editor commending each for his years as the principal of one of Galveston's public schools.

McKee Andrus

Andrus retired as the principal of William B. Travis Elementary School about seven years after June 17, 1963, the day the U.S. Supreme Court ruled that reverential Bible reading and prayer recitation are unconstitutional in our public schools.

For the nearly two hundred years prior to that, Andrus and Smart and their counterparts nationwide, had begun each school day with a randomly selected student reciting a prayer before his schoolmates.

In the later years, "May I have your attention, please?" would come over the classrooms' loudspeakers. The children and teachers would stand, face the flag and recite the Pledge of Allegiance. Next a student would deliver a prayer. All would then sit quietly while the principal and a handful of others would give announcements about upcoming PTA and student council meetings and that year's Little Olympics tryouts.

In 1787, the delegates of the thirteen original states convened in Philadelphia to draft a set of rules for self-government, the Constitution. When they took it home for the vote of the people, they found many of their constituents outraged. The Constitution made great efforts to say what the federal government could do, but it said little about what the federal government couldn't do. The Constitution might not have been ratified without the promise of a bill of rights.

So the First Congress of the United States (1789-1791) drafted the ten amendments to the Constitution which became known as The Bill of Rights. This was approved by the necessary three-quarters of the states and became a part of the Constitution on December 15, 1791.

The Constitution established our democracy. Democracy means that people can vote for their public officials in fair elections and that a vote of the majority will make most political decisions.

The Bill of Rights, on the other hand, gives Americans liberty. Liberty means those rights the government or majority can never take away. The Bill of Rights guarantees man the protection of his human dignity. Those rights, as a whole, are often referred to as "unalienable rights," "natural rights," and "the great rights of mankind."

They include the right to have a religion or not to have one, free from government influence or compulsion; the right to unpopular expression, a privilege that government can't take away or censor; freedom from governmental intrusion into your private affairs; the right of a fair trial should your liberty ever be at stake; and the right to be treated fairly, regardless of social status, religion, color or national origin.

So doesn't it seem odd that although the public was outraged that the framers would first present the Constitution to them without a bill of rights, it would take nearly 175 years for anyone to seriously challenge what was apparently the majority's unspoken interpretation of a particular one of those rights?

It seems even more incongruous to those of us who had school principals like Andrus and Smart, that they would have allowed anything to take place in their schools that they considered a violation of one's rights, whether or not that right was specifically protected by law.

Could it have been that they found school prayer one more way students could learn about each other; one more way in which the limp rope of universal tolerance could be pushed toward a goal reasonable people share, being able to understand one another?

Could it have been that the students and teachers were asked to be silent during the student's prayer out of respect for the student, and not for the purpose of displaying any acceptance or directing any reverence to the deity to whom his prayer was being addressed?

Was anyone ever denied the right to pray to, or not to pray to, whomever or whatever he chose, when the lottery chose the student's name? Was he prevented from saying, instead of delivering a prayer, "We will now have two minutes of silence?"

In the spring of 1951, my friend Ronnie delivered a Jewish prayer one morning just prior to Andrus' announcements. After Ronnie came back to the classroom, Rosemarie asked why he hadn't mentioned Jesus in his prayer.

The teacher, Louise Hayes, suggested that Ronnie answer Rosemarie's question by preparing for the class a presentation on the Jewish beliefs and traditions. Ronnie thought it would be a good idea if Doris, Errol and Marlene, who were also Jewish, worked with him. Mrs. Hayes agreed.

So when the day came for Ronnie, Errol, Marlene and Doris' presentation, Ronnie brought a Torah to class. He explained that a Torah is a scroll that holds the first five books of Moses (Genesis, Exodus, Leviticus, Numbers and Deuteronomy) written in Hebrew. The Torah, he said, contains the basis of Jewish knowledge.

He showed us that it is written in Hebrew with Hebrew characters, and that Hebrew, unlike English, is read from the bottom of the page up, right to left.

Errol explained that when a Jewish boy becomes thirteen, he is "bar mitzvahed." Marlene added that it is a relatively new tradition for a girl to be "bas mitzvahed." The sum total of both of those ceremonies is to acknowledge that the child has been formally exposed to and is committed to the 613 good-deed commandments in the Torah, called "mitzvahs." Mitzvahs are the commandments by which Jews are expected to live their lives.

"You've heard of Mogen David Wine?" Doris asked. "That wine is named after the six-pointed star called the Mogen David. I wear one around my neck. It is to Jews what the cross is to some of you. It is a symbol of our religion."

There is nothing more insidious to a society than some of its members having a lack of tolerance for one another. There is nothing more destructive to reaching toward a universally agreed-on goal of a perfect civilization than that civilization's people having to continually swim in a sea poisoned by the venom of intolerance for some.

It's not hard to understand that one person, one group or one entity trying to involve people in a particular religious belief through a governmental venue, is against the Bill of Rights.

It is quite another thing, though, to profess the belief that we are better off by preventing our schools from saying to a kid, "We're going to give you two minutes to demonstrate before us something you think we should know about you. We are going to honor you by remaining silent and paying attention while you do it."

If he shows us a magic trick, introduces us to his dog, Sam, or delivers a prayer that is meaningful to him, it seems evident that through that display, we will have acquired at least one more sliver of knowledge, however minuscule, of whom he and those like him are.

That is, after all, what occurred 1951, when Ronnie prayed, Rosemarie asked why he didn't mention Jesus, and Mrs. Hayes made sure twenty-six children were properly exposed to a culture and religion called Judaism.

Business

The Story of Sam's Galveston Gold Mine

If you or your family have been Galveston residents for at least fifty years, it is almost a certainty that your surname has appeared on at least one, probably many more than one, bicycle invoices from Sam Bazaman's bike shop, West End Cycle.

Sam was born and educated here, and when he got out of high school the war was going on, so like it did for so many others, it put his plans on hold.

When the war was over and he came back to the island, he returned with only two goals, and both would come to be very important to that which comprised Sam's adult life. The first was to go in hot pursuit of his love interest, Yetta Kreisler, and the other was to open a bike shop.

So every weekend when Sam got off work, he got on his motorcycle and drove up old Texas Highway 75 to Dallas, then took 77 to Denton, some 375 miles all-told, where Yetta was a student at Texas Women's College. When Sunday came, he'd do the whole thing in reverse in order to be at work in Galveston on Monday morning.

With that kind of tenacity, it was no wonder Yetta said yes when Sam asked her to marry him. Then Sam was ready to work toward accomplishing his second goal, the bike shop.

Sam and Yetta opened their new venture under an old house at 721 37th, on the north side of Broadway. There were a bunch of bike shops here in those days. The Rasmussen family had one, so did Tom Sedgwick, and there was K & L on 28th Street.

Now old man J.E. Meyers was senior vice president of U.S. National Bank then, and Sam banked there, as did his family, and, in fact, as did Yetta's family. Meyers had a son, Ralph, who was about seven, and who was named after his brother Ralph who a big wig with International Creosoting & Construction Co. Both brothers were proud of being close with a dollar. It was, afterall, a family tradition that stretched back at least three generations.

So as you might guess, now that Old Man Meyers' son Ralph was ready for his first bike, he was bought a used bike rather than a new one. And thereafter on most Saturday afternoons, as regular as clockwork, Old Man Meyers would bring the bike in for repairs. This week it would be a broken link on the chain, the next week one of the old tires would be flat. He'd sit in an old office chair Sam and Yetta had in the shop that he'd positioned under the big ceiling fan so he could keep cool while Sam made the repairs.

Remembering Sam's bent for being tenacious, as you would expect, each week Sam would try to sell him a new bike for Ralph rather than repair the old one. Every week Old Man Meyers would continue the family tradition and tell Sam to just fix the old one.

It became a predictable part of their friendship for Old Man Meyers to exclaim whenever he saw Sam, whether it was while getting Ralph's bike fixed or in the bank when Sam came to make a deposit, "Sam, you've got a gold mine. You've really got a gold mine!"

Now Sam's business continued to grow, meanwhile he and Yetta had two boys and a girl, but they also knew the importance of saving to build their business. Finally Sam and Yetta decided they had just enough money for a down payment to buy the property and build a big and modern bike shop near 39th and Broadway where the shop is today.

Sam and Yetta knew they would need a loan, but they had only heard about how one borrows money from a bank, they had never actually done it before.

Sam made an appointment with his friend, J.E. Meyers, he put on his suit and tie, and he went in to see him about making a loan for his new bike shop. Old Man Meyers listened intently and without saying a word, and then when Sam was finished with his request for the loan, Old Man Meyers said, "Sam, you know when you make a bank loan you have to have collateral. What do you and Yetta propose to use for collateral?"

"Sam's gold mine, Mr. Meyers. Sam's gold mine," was the reply.

Old Man Meyers leaned back in his chair, chuckled, then came forward, handed Sam the Esterbrook pen from his desk set, filled with blue-black ink banks preferred and said, "Sign here, Sam."

Jim Woodall's Contributions to the Island and Its People Live After Him

Jim Woodall

The USS Cavalla has been a museum to World War II submarine veterans since it was first parked at Seawolf Park's shore edge in 1972. In recent months, officials of the parks board and the U.S. Submarine Veterans of World War II sparred over how to rectify its now dilapidated condition.

Many of us hoped the Cavalla would be returned to being a well-kept monument, but not primarily for the reasons you might think. Our wish was for it to remain as the personal legacy of former American National Insurance Co. assistant vice president, James A. Woodall.

Let me describe Woodall for those of you who didn't know him. He was a snappy dresser—new suits, ties, shoes and hats every season from Walter Pye's. He was how actor James Cagney would have looked, walked, talked and acted had the good Lord not had other more important things on his mind the day he created Cagney.

Woodall liked people. People liked Woodall.

He began his career in the insurance business as an office boy with Reserve Loan Life in Dallas, advancing through the ranks until he enlisted in the Navy in World War II. He trained as a member of the ground crew for naval aviation, but shortly thereafter volunteered for submarine duty.

He was aboard the Tender U.S. Griggin in the Philippines when the war ended.

Woodall returned to Reserve Loan Life, and was brought to Galveston when the company was bought by American National. W. L. Vogler and R. A. Furbush were running ANICO then.

As time past, Woodall became the division manager over a number of the company's insurance policy administrative departments. He also married Kay, who was Vogler's executive assistant.

It was in the early 1970s that Woodall decided it was time for him to make his mark. He began to spend countless hours working to convince local and national authorities that a World War II submarine should be bought and made into a museum. That museum should be placed at Galveston's Seawolf Park.

Woodall saw it as a memorial to the many veterans who had been in the submarine service. He saw it as a money making attraction for Galveston.

Now at that same time, a girl from the mainland, who was just out of high school, was sent to him by the ANICO personnel department to work as a file clerk in one his departments. It was her first job. She was overly shy and unsure of herself.

Like today, back then prospective employees took employment tests. At ANICO, everyone other than file clerks and maintenance people were required to pass a typing test, irrespective of whether or not typing was a part of the position's job description.

The girl didn't pass the typing test when she applied for a job.

Over time, Woodall observed the job performance of his new employee, and he began to question how she ended up in a position he felt was far below her intellect and qualifications. He called her in. She said she never did well on tests because she was always afraid she'd fail. He told her that the only part of the battery of tests she had done poorly on was typing competency. He said he thought he could get the personnel department to let her retake that part of the test.

Now Woodall was a salesman and a convincing salesman at that. Somehow he sold friends he had in the company's personnel department to get him a copy of the typing test and lend him a typewriter. He put them in the trunk of his car. They didn't know what he planned to do with them.

That afternoon he told the girl to bring her car to the company's parking lot. He had something he wanted to put in it for her. It was too big and too heavy to deliver some other way. The bell rang at 4:30, the girl followed her boss' instructions, and he loaded the borrowed typewriter in her trunk and gave her the typing test.

"Go home and practice and practice until you can type this thing at a speed of at least sixty words a minute," he told her. "Never tell anyone you had the test in advance."

Shortly thereafter, he made arrangements for his clerk to retake the typing test. When the day came, she passed with flying colors. Woodall immediately promoted her.

Now before you take a critical position of Woodall's handling of this matter, let me tell you that the job Woodall had in mind for the girl was one that required math skills and the ability to learn the complexities of insurance. He knew she had that. Being able to type sixty words a minute had nothing to do with either.

Woodall's rationalization was that the girl was the best qualified for that analytical position, and that by her being promoted into it, that was what was best for both the company and her.

Over the following twenty-five years, Woodall's gentle push and belief in his employee were the foundation that helped her build the self-confidence she needed to become the extremely successful business woman that she is today as a Strand storeowner.

Jim Woodall always knew how to tinker with the "It can't be done" mentality to bring good things to the world around him. The USS Cavalla's service to Galveston and his former employee's successes are just two of the examples.

A Lesson to the Man Who Tried to Call the Banker a Crook

Recently the family of Douglas D. Lee, president for many years and later chairman of Bank of Galveston, celebrated the anniversary of his death with a well-written memorial in the paper.

Everyone who knew Lee has a favorite story about him, and each one thinks his particular story is the best. I would like to submit mine to the scrutiny and the vote.

The telephone rang, and the operator told Lee that there was a very upset man on the line who was calling from Alaska, and was yelling something about fraud and law suits and jail time. He was demanding to speak to Lee right then.

A lifelong sufferer from various Galveston breeds of allergies, Lee said he would certainly take the call, but he'd have to blow his nose, cough, wheeze, sneeze and clear his throat a few times before he'd be able to speak to the man, and it would have to be all right with me, since the caller would, after all, be interrupting our conference.

After these nasal acrobatics and with the formality

of my permission, but without any sign of concern about charges of fraud, law suits, jail time or whatever, he picked up the phone, and here's the end of the conversation I heard.

"Well, how're you, Joe . . . I read in the paper that Mr. Sam died. Fine man and a good friend. I surely am sorry. Be sure you tell your mom she's in our prayers.

"You know, I didn't know he'd been living up there in Alaska. I lost track of him after he married your mom. When was that . . . about six or seven years ago, now, wasn't it?

"He did what? Well I had no idea he had named me the beneficiary of that $100,000 Life-Paid-Up-at-65 policy he bought back in the 60s from Leroy Brown. I knew he'd bought it because he came by here to set up the bank draft, but that was long before Miss Olive, you know his first wife, died.

"You sure I'm the beneficiary? The insurance company told your mom that, did they? Well, now you know I'll bet I know what happened. Mr. Sam's and Miss Olive's only child was Bobby, and he was shot down and killed in Viet Nam. Right thereafter, Miss Olive got breast cancer and after a long struggle, died. Mr. Sam was single and by himself for a quite a time. I worried about him. Before he met your mom, he'd come by here every morning for coffee and we'd visit.

"Anyway, I'll bet he just decided to change the beneficiary on that policy to name me 'cuz he needed someone to settle up his bills and stuff when he died because when Miss Olive passed away, he had no one left in his family.

He never told me about doing it, though, not that it would have mattered because I would have known what I was suppose to do with the money.

"In any case, it was some years later that he married your mom, and he probably just forgot to change the beneficiary designation to her. May have even not given much thought to the policy since he had long since completed paying the premiums. What was he, about seventy-eight or so when he died? That'd have been thirteen years since it was paid up.

"Tell your mom not to worry. As soon as the check comes over here to the bank, I'll endorse it, get it cleared and send her a cashier's check for it. Give me that address."

After Lee hung up he said, "I think that fellow thought I had talked his stepfather into making me the beneficiary of his policy so I could get the money. I can't imagine why he would think that."

I said, "Mr. Lee, that guy doesn't know you, and maybe it wasn't so hard for him to jump to that conclusion. After all, I wonder how many other bankers have ever had a customer name them the beneficiary of their life policy, trusting them to use that money to settle their estate for them, especially when you consider that Mr. Sam didn't even tell you he had done it nor did he instruct you as to how you were to disburse the money?"

Lee responded, "I don't know, but that sort of thing happens to me all of the time."

"Mr. Lee simply doesn't get it," I thought. This is

the same man who for years did the entire bank's payroll each payday by himself, hand-writing the checks, to make certain that each payday he would consciously and singularly evaluate each employee, and if it was time to reward one with a raise, he'd just do it right then. He saw no sense in waiting until an anniversary date.

During his lifetime, few who worked for Douglas D. Lee could imagine quitting to work for someone else, so they didn't. His customers couldn't imagine banking with anyone else either, so they didn't. The influence and teaching of D.D. Lee is still a major influence over the way business is transacted at the Bank of Galveston, and that's as it should be. Good morals always make a solid foundation.

The Purity Ice Cream Factory and the Ten O'Clock Valve

A few years ago the Jack King family bought the Purity Ice Cream Co., its real estate at 12th and Avenue E, and its equipment and recipes from the estate of G. B. Brynston. Their reason for the acquisition was to be able to manufacture ice cream for their popular Strand business, La King's Confectionary.

Laura Elder, then a reporter for the Houston Business Journal, wrote in a front page article that Purity would soon resume manufacturing ice cream to be sold elsewhere, perhaps up to the 5,000 gallons a month the factory made and sold when Brynston was the owner.

Like Blue Bell ice cream, until it closed, Purity was so popular in Galveston County that few drugstore soda fountains or neighborhood grocery stores carried any other brand. In fact all of the public school cafeterias had it in individual cup servings with little wooden spoons.

The ice cream was high in butter fat and was, in the main, flavored with natural ingredients like real strawberries, and it was always fresh, so you can imagine it started the taste race far ahead of its competition.

At special times of the year like Christmas and New Year's, seasonal flavors arrived like peppermint and egg nog. In addition to the normal favorites—vanilla, chocolate and strawberry—butter pecan was the most popular. The King family won't have any trouble whatsoever in getting testimony from oldtime locals that not even Blue Bell has approached the goodness of Brynston's Purity.

In addition to his famous ice cream, Brynston, although a quiet behind-the-scenes kind of businessman, was an astute marketer. Drugstore soda fountains were major sources of ice cream sales in those days, and there were an enormous number of family owned neighborhood drugstores throughout the county. In fact in Galveston of the forty drugstores, only Walgreen's at 22nd and Postoffice was owned by a national firm.

To not only get the account but assure allegiance, Brynston would supply at Purity's cost the soda fountain ice cream freezers and would provide the store's fancy outside neon sign with the name of the store on top and Purity's name below. And when cash flow was short for the drugstore owner, he could depend on quietly making a very low interest rate, unsecured loan with Brynston to get the store over the hump.

For years Brynston resisted installing an automatic valve on a certain piece of equipment at the factory, and no matter what, according to Brynston, that valve had to be manually turned off at exactly ten o'clock each evening. He claimed it was not only impossible but silly to expect to find a regular employee who would sit in the plant from five o'clock in the afternoon until ten o'clock that evening with the sole duty of turning off that valve.

So Brynston set up a couple of top loaded freezers in the plant's front office and a counter where people in the neighborhood could come in and buy a pint, quart or half gallon of freshly made ice cream. To handle the sales and the turning off of that important valve at exactly ten o'clock, he hired school teachers, a different one to work each night.

His pitch to the teachers was that they could grade papers and make money at the same time. But more importantly, in those days if school employees contributed to Social Security as well as the manditory Teachers' Retirement, they were elegible to draw both when they retired. Brynston's plan gave those teachers like Riley H. Lefevers, George W. Bertschler, William O. Barlow and Arthur L. Graham, who moonlighted with Purity, that extra advantage.

I concluded long ago that Brynston purposely chose not to automate that valve, and that decision had nothing whatsoever to do with the ice cream manufacturing business. And further, maybe it didn't even need to be turned off at exactly ten o'clock each night. It seems much more likely to me that the whole thing was a dignified scheme to help teachers.

G. B. Brynston was like that.

Y2K Has Little on 1960

The world seemed to be terribly concerned about what computers are going to do when the calendar rolled over to the year of 2000. Apparently many of those who wrote the programs never contemplated that the programs or the computers would be in use on January 1, 2000, a rather odd conculsion for an industry whose whole premise was showing us the future.

But then this same kind of thing happened about forty years ago to the old W. L. Moody & Co., Bankers, Unincorporated, when the world moved from 1959, into 1960, but it was for an entirely different reason. The Burroughs bookkeeping machines which kept track of and printed the customers' statements each month had only been made to last for twenty-five years. The problem W. L. Moody & Co., Bankers, was facing was that twenty-five years for their machines had started in 1934.

Ironically, Burroughs thought the actual technology of their machines was everlasting because they felt it unimprovable. To counteract that, the company decided not to manufacturer a part that would allow those machines to print 1960, or any year thereafter, for that matter. In the business world, everyone calls this "planned obsolescence."

In 1959, W. L. Moody & Co., Bankers, was being run by A. V. Stjepcevich, Robert W. "Buddy" Burgess, Lester Schott, Leo Ritzler and D. D. Lee. Robert Houston was the head teller, and had hopes of soon being an officer. They had all been brought up in that bank by W. L. Moody, Jr., and even though Moody had been dead for five years by 1959, they continued to do their best at running the bank exactly as he had taught them.

So the question facing them now was, How would Mr. Moody handle this problem of the bookkeeping machines? After all, the old machines worked fine. The one and only problem was each had an obsolete date wheel, and the manufacturer was not providing a replacement because it wanted to sell the banks new, but quite frankly, at least in this case, unneeded machines.

Now in those days, since W. L. Moody & Co., Bankers, was not a national bank, it was required to use Moody National Bank to clear checks deposited by customers that were drawn on other banks. As cashier for W. L. Moody & Co.,Bankers, handling the bank's daily clearings was one of Buddy Burgess' responsibilities.

One day about noon, in fact about this time of the year in 1959, it was raining terribly. When Burgess went up to the south balcony at Moody National where the clearing took place everyday, he saw proof operators Gina Filidei and Sylvia Mazzantini had big sheets of plastic on top of their proof machines, and umbrellas tied to their chairs. They were working under those umbrellas, trying to stay dry, for water was pouring in from the leaking roof, and it was obvious to Burgess that the roof had been leaking for a long time. That bank had also been owned and operated by W. L. Moody, Jr.

That brought to mind what Moody had said to all of his employees so many times, "Whenever you spend a dollar, you spend a friend." They had their answer. W. L. Moody would not have replaced the bookeeping machines; he would have improvised instead, and thus kept a bunch of his "friends."

Putting their heads together, Stjepcevich, Burgess, Schott and Ritzler came up with a very simple and workable plan, a plan Moody would have been proud of them for: The bookeeping clerks would simply alter the dates each month on the statements with a ballpoint pen, so that when the statements were sent to the customers, they reflected the proper year, 1960.

W. L. Moody & Co., Bankers, has long been out of business, but at 90, Robert W. "Buddy" Burgess was still here to tell the stories of the bank and of Galveston. In fact, there is not one person alive on this planet who can say he traded at W. L. Moody & Co., Bankers, when Burgess wasn't an employee there. He went there in 1922, when he was fourteen. He retired in 1969, after forty-seven years, but within moments went to work at Moody National Bank, in their new building. He spent another twelve years there.

I knew Buddy Burgess and his wife, Lucille, for my entire life. The last time I saw Buddy Burgess, I asked him how old he was. "Ninety," he said. "Don't you think that's too long for anyone to live," he mused? My answer was, "Nope! And most certainly not in your case."

So it was appropriate that the Mary Moody Northen Foundation gave a scholarship to Galveston College in Buddy Burgess' name. Like many employees of what was then known as "The House of Moody," he brought and gave a lifetime of honor to the businesses of Galveston's Moody family. That's one powerful legacy, and the scholarship was one powerful way to acknowledge that legacy.

Galveston Characters

1947: Galveston Hosts National Happy Hermits Political Convention

He changed his shirt with the same frequency that he changed his tattoos. That he was a hermit was more the result of his hygiene habits than that he didn't care to be around people.

Those who knew him called him Frenchy. His parents had named him Clesmey N. LeBlanc. The average person on the Island referred to him as the "crazy hermit who lives on the concrete ship."

Christie "the Beachcomber" Mitchell, whose powerful exclamation to everyone was, "Baby, I'm going to make you a star," was the most creative publicist the island ever had. He decided he could bring nationwide notoriety to Galveston by making Frenchy a star.

Frenchy lived on the USS Selma, a ship that had been sunk in six feet of water off the coast of Pelican Island. It remains there today.

The USS Selma was one of twelve concrete ships the government decided to build during World War I to conserve steel. They were built on the east coast and to be oil tankers. They cost about $2 million each.

On its maiden voyage, the Selma went to Tampico. As it was arriving, its captain got off course and drove the boat over a jetty, puncturing its bottom, and causing its hold to fill with water, and the vessel to go aground.

Planks were nailed to the bottom as a temporary patch. She was then bailed out and towed to Galveston's Pier 35 for permanent repairs. A hurricane came into the gulf, and the Selma's new captain, Edward Howell, moved the ship under its own power to a safer place, Pier 10.

Some months later, in 1923, marine engineers concluded that she could not be repaired to be seaworthy. Again Capt. Howell fired-up the boat's steam engines, and moved her to her final resting place where she was run aground.

In 1947, Frenchy LeBlanc bought the USS Selma. LeBlanc paid its then-owner, Henry Dalehite's Galvez Boat Service, one hundred bucks for it. Some say he did it in ten dollar a month installments.

Frenchy, whose only teeth were those that had been given him by Dr. W. L. Glenn, Sr., had a bad leg which kept him from getting a good, full-time job.

There was no welfare or public assistance of consequence in those days. and there was no permanent public subsidized housing. Frenchy decided that with his impairment, he could no longer afford high rent, women, taxes, or food from the grocery store, and he was certain no one was going to provide them free for him.

The first solution he considered was to build a house boat for himself; however, he realized he wouldn't be able to collect enough free lumber to do that. He decided that his best option was to buy the Selma. He could live in its cabin, fish from its deck, raise a goat or two and a handful of chickens on board, and sell day-passes to those who were curious about him, and who wanted to fish there. The enterprise worked.

As the ferry boats passed, the passengers saw Frenchy fishing off of the ship's deck. They'd wave. Sometimes he'd wave back; other times he wouldn't. The ferry-boat deck-hands were certain that if you saw Frenchy wave, he was waving at the porpoises that were rolling above the water; he wasn't waving at you.

In the Indian Summer of 1947, Christie Mitchell was the public relations person for the Greater Galveston Beach Association. Looking for a publicity angle for the island, he convinced Frenchy to found a bogus third political party—Happy Hermits. The club's first national convention would be held on the deck of the Selma, and the delegates would sit on three wash-tubs, four oyster crates and some makeshift driftwood benches. Their primary business would be to elect their own United States presidential candidate.

Large, cloth two-man banners on poles were made so they could be held up by the conventioneers for the ferry passengers to read: "We seek solution from intrusion." "Civilization? We'll stay in Galveston!" "We need women delegates. All applicants preapproved."

While Mitchell's claim was that the club members and convention delegates were hermit lifestyle sympathizers from Florida, Colorado, Maine, Michigan, New York, Arizona and elsewhere in Texas, in reality, they were his regular drinking buddies from Johnny Jack's club in the Marine Building on 21st and Mechanic Street.

It's a fact that a couple of those "delegates" were other Galveston characters. Lionel Pellerin, for an example. He was the dapper, handsome and admired maitre d' at the Balinese Room.

Robert Kennedy was there as well. He was a character of the same dynamic as Frenchy and known as Safety Santa. He was in his "dress" Santa uniform—a purple suit with gold braiding, and a big felt cowboy hat with a red, white and blue plume. Of course he also sported his trademark eighteen-inch white beard.

And there was Blind Tom Ragusa. He was the legendary and frequently subpoenaed defense witness who would predictably testify that he saw nothing, allowing the jury reason to let the scoundrel go free.

Somehow Mitchell convinced Movietone News and Universal News that the whole "convention" was on the up-and-up—a true and serious news event, not a promotion gimmick. They sent cameras to film the occasion.

Back then, newsreels were shown before every movie. In the newsreel Happy Hermits segments, viewers saw the delegates holding the club's "platform" banners, then Frenchy declining the nomination to be the club's first presidential candidate. Then they saw resolution: Safety Santa then being nominated and unanimously winning his bid as the Happy Hermits' presidential candidate.

Galveston Memories

Lee Orr of Fox Movietone estimated that in excess of twenty million movie goers learned about Galveston, the "Playground of the Southwest."

It's interesting to note that shortly before the first Happy Hermits national convention was organized, the U.S. Army Corps of Engineers gave Houston's Harrisburg Machine Co. a permit to board the Selma, stack lumber from another wrecked boat on her deck, and burn it. This was apparently done without Frenchy's permission.

Mitchell had helped Frenchy find an attorney, another character in his own right, a fellow named Michael Kustoff. Kustoff claimed to be a white Russian who, before he had immigrated to Galveston, had been a captain of the Cossacks.

Kustoff's pleadings for LeBlanc claimed that the fire Harrisburg Machine Co. had built on the Selma's deck had caused enormous cracks in the area of the ship's cabin, making the vessel unsafe. The damages LeBlanc sought from Harrisburg were $1,000 and a public apology.

Naturally, because of this association and sympathy, Kustoff also was a delegate at the first Happy Hermits political convention.

The Selma, sans Frenchy, remains today in its final resting place. The Selma is now owned by a former reporter for the Galveston Daily News, Pat Daniels. That is appropriate, since Daniels appears to be a character in his own right. Each year he holds an on-land birthday party for the Selma. Entertainment for the guests is provided by a huge kazoo band.

Monk and the Bartender Set the Clock Back for the Alibi

There are people like Monk everywhere. They are small-time hoods who come to town out of nowhere, charm a few girls, give away a few phony diamond rings, become engaged to be married at least three times, and take contracts on the lives of a few cronies, all before they go on the lam.

Monk was so good at lying and charming that one time he served as a pallbearer at a guy's funeral who, two afternoons before, he had rubbed out. And Monk cried up a storm, dabbing his eyes with his silk pocket handkerchief while Saint Patrick Church's Father John Murphy gave the eulogy.

There was a combination bar and deli where the good and the bad used to mix for drinks, lunch and discussion. Since no one had figured out how to make an inexpensive wristwatch shock-proof, most men used pocket watches. Rather than fiddle around trying to get their watches out, it was habit to check the bar's wall clock.

On this particular afternoon, Monk had taken a contract on the life of a fellow who worked as a cotton grader by day, and philandered on his wife by night. And wouldn't you know that there was a subplot: For at least a year, Monk and the cotton grader's wife had been sneaking off to Monk's room at the old Panama Hotel.

The guy who put the contract out with Monk was the woman's father, and he was also the bartender at the combination bar and deli.

When a hit-man is hired, the most important part of the equation, other than not missing when he shoots, is having the alibi planned. So Monk and the bartender came up with this one:

Just before the bar was to open, the bartender would set the clock on the wall back an hour. Monk would later make an entrance, sit at the bar with his cronies for awhile, then nonchalantly look at the wall clock and say, "It's one o'clock. I've gotta get outta here." And with that, everyone in ear-shot would look up at the wall clock and think to themselves, "Yep, it's one o'clock, all right." Nobody would pull out his pocket watch to see it was really two o'clock.

Monk would then leave, go bump off the bartender's son-in-law, then come back and say, "I put twenty bucks on Greased Supreme to place in the third race." Then he would add parenthetically, "Would you believe it? It's already one forty-five."

Of course the idea was that everyone in the bar would have to say, should anybody ask, that Monk was sitting at the bar at time the murder took place.

Well, the bartender and Monk followed the plan just

like they had agreed. Monk had even placed the bet with Harry the Hat moments before he put a silenced bullet through the right temple of the philanderer.

When Monk came back to the bar, he and attorney Marsene Johnson walked in at the same time, and not only did Johnson have on his expensive, shock-proof, gold Elgin wristwatch, but moments before he had checked to see if it agreed with the clock above the door at the United States National Bank. It had.

When Johnson and Monk went into the bar, Johnson mused to the bartender, "You know your clock is an hour slow?" Those sitting at the bar pulled out their pocket watches. All agreed with Johnson, and without anyone then being the wiser, other than the bartender and Monk, Monk's alibi vanished, just like that. The bartender moved the clock up an hour.

With the alibi gone, the bartender was afraid to pay off the contract to Monk. He knew that the chances were the cops would eventually figure out that Monk had killed the bartender's son-in-law, and that if even the slightest circumstantial evidence showed the bartender to have been involved, he would be convicted as an accessory.

Meanwhile, the son-in-law had to be buried. So, in order to further throw the cops off the trail, the bartender suggested to his daughter that Monk should be one of the pallbearers.

The daughter, now thinking that soon she and Monk would no longer have to meet in private, and further, sure that she was in love with Monk, agreed. She thought Monk's presence at the funeral would bring her comfort.

So the funeral came, and that's when Monk cried and dabbed his eyes on his silk hanky. Afterwards, he went to collect on his contract. The bartender refused to pay. Monk was furious. It was his first contract to go bad in his professional life as a hit-man. And he was about to be out the five hundred buck contract fee, too.

Meanwhile, the detectives heard about the bar clock having been an hour behind. They started interviewing those who had been there. They learned Monk was one of them.

At their usual time, a few days after the funeral and before the police had caught up with Monk, he showed up at the new widow's house, rather than her coming to his room at the Panama.

After she had disrobed and gotten into bed, he came into the bedroom and blew her brains out, just like that.

Then he went to the combination bar and deli for a drink and some chitchat with his cronies. He said, "It's already four o'clock. Where's the day gone?" Everybody looked at their pocket watches this time, and sure enough, it was four o'clock.

The next morning the bartender discovered his daughter's dead, naked body in her bed. When the police came to investigate, they found every clock in her house was running exactly an hour behind. That forced the bartender to have to give Monk his alibi by saying that Monk had been with him at the time of his daughter's murder.

No one ever saw Monk again The word was that he moved to Chicago where a smart hit-man could make an honest living.

When Safety Santa Arrived at Perusina's, Only McCoy Farqua was Caught by Surprise

The waitress had just taken theater man Johnny Browning's order for a minute steak, medium rare, with sides of mashed potatoes and fresh butter beans, and a large glass of iced tea with the customary two sprigs of mint.

He was sitting at a table near the cash register at Perusina's, a restaurant that back then was at 2114 Mechanic Street, next door to the Galveston Daily News building. And this was long before Clara Biggers became the cafe's most popular waitress.

At the table to his left, Galveston Daily News reporter Lillian Herz, was down to her bread pudding, and was alternating spoonfuls with drags on her Lucky Strike. As usual, she had on her black crepe dress with the long skirt and her Louella Parson's hat. The way she was dressed along with her nicotine stained nose was a dead give-away that she was a newspaper woman.

Dallasite McCoy Farqua was mindlessly putting nickel after nickel into a slot machine while waiting for his blue plate special when he heard a choir of diners say "Hi, Robert!"

Even though he figured the chances of knowing Robert were slim, nevertheless Farqua looked toward the door, and at that very moment he and everyone else heard these words of shock pour from his mouth, "Who is that?"

And almost as soon as he heard them himself, he realized that out of the hundred or so men, women and the few children who were in the dining room, he was the only one surprised.

Now this was a Thursday, and it was the second week of July, and I might as well tell you that the person named Robert who had garnered the one surprise and the ninety-nine nonchalant hellos was fully dressed in a red wool Santa Claus outfit, down to the long white beard which was very obviously his.

In place of the customary red stocking cap, though, he had on what appeared to be a white drum major's hat; one of those cylindrical affairs that is every bit a foot tall with a black bill at the bottom, and with all of the gold braiding running up and down it and with a red feather plume flaring out of the top, all held on his head by a black leather strap under his chin.

Now remember, air conditioning was scarce in those days, and the temperature outside was approaching ninety. Nevertheless, Kennedy was in his red wool Santa Claus suit with the white drum major hat, and only McCoy Farqua from Dallas on that day and at that time found the scene unusual.

Galveston Memories

Galvestonians were used to Robert Kennedy, a man who called himself Safety Santa Claus, and who spent at least forty years voluntarily giving safety programs in the schools, and who, in the summertime, stood in the hot sun at the entrance of Murdoch's Bath House day after day to instruct tourists on gulf water safety.

Just as today bubbas and cowboys are never seen in public without their hats, for after all they are playing a part, Robert Kennedy was never seen without his Santa Claus suit.

He was born in Canada in 1873, and got to Galveston by ship in 1923. He went to work as an agent for the Prudential Insurance Co., but that profession just wasn't for him. Because his family were Scots, they had taught Robert and his ten siblings about farming. So it wasn't long after he got to Galveston that he decided he'd probably be a better farmer than an insurance salesman.

He went to work on a farm in Hitchcock, and later moved to a farm in Dickinson.

In those days, it wasn't illegal in Texas to let cattle roam and graze wherever they pleased. Prior to highways, cars and trucks, if you think about it, there wasn't much need to fence pastures. But now things were different. There were cars and trucks and paved highways. Seeing the dangers free roaming livestock posed to motorists, Robert took it upon himself to try to get the state legislature to pass laws requiring fencing.

As a result, outraged farmers made every effort to run him out of the county. At least one person threatened his life if he didn't give up his quest. So although Robert never left Dickinson, he quickly changed his agenda by becoming Safety Santa Claus reigning over all of Galveston County.

During his many years as Safety Santa, he received letters of thanks from police chief Fred Ford, governor Coke Stevenson, superintendent of education Kathleen Bradford Benson, movie star Shirley Temple, Eleanor Roosevelt and Chamber of Commerce's E. Sid Holliday, plus from scores of others you've never heard of.

And all during the years of World War II, Safety Santa headed the War Savings Bond Program for Galveston County and at his side were the famous quadruplet daughters of the Ellis Badgetts, Joan, Jeraldine, Jennette and Joyce.

Oh, and I forgot to tell you. Safety Santa Claus was tall and skinny so when he added the drum major hat, he was over eight feet tall. He didn't look like the Santa Claus you know, but on that day in July at Perusina's, apparently only McCoy Farqua noticed.

Memories

Friends Archie Crow and Leroy Brown Got Together One Last Time

The News said Archie M. Crow, Jr. "went to be with the Lord, Thursday, August 5, 1999." He breathed his last breath in Trinity, Texas, where he and his wife lived.

Archie Crow was my friend as was his son, Archie, III. And while I found a lump in my throat as I read what for me was an unanticipated obituary, I found myself smiling at the end of it, where a subtle irony had been left for those who knew him.

In the 1950s and 1960s when the Crows still lived in Galveston, Archie Crow took Nick and Mary Ballich's old and famous Elite Cafe and the adjacent Ping-Pong Club of Albert Doveri, remodeled them, and created a fine seafood restaurant, a drive-in where Seawall Mary worked from time to time, and a private night club called the Crow's Nest. On that very same site and in that very same building, today, stands Joe's Crab Shack.

For the opening of the Crow's Nest, Archie Crow recruited the famed bartender from the Balinese Room, Santos Cruz, as the club's manager; the gracious Ralph

Martin, the head waiter at the old downtown Lloyd's Club; and a popular saloon singer and bar room piano player named George Bushong from Dorothy Graham's Metropole Club.

Each one of them had his own following, so the Crow's Nest was an instant success. It was the place to go, the place to be seen. If you were a member of the in-crowd in those days, you had two membership cards in your pocket—one for Gaido's Pelican Club, the other for the Crow's Nest.

State Theater's Johnny Browning frequently stopped by and took a stool at the piano bar, where he eventually would be encouraged to sing, "Ace in the Hole." Charles Garbelich, who had been the maitre d' at the old Sportsman Club before it was torched and burned to the ground, was always seated next to Browning. Garbelich never missed singing, in his thick "wherever" foreign country accent, a song with a ridiculous story titled, "Hello, Central."

Galveston beauties like Mary Helen Bovio, Juliet Papi and Diane Vento, with their dates, were often on stools nearby.

Meanwhile, the requests and the tip jar would mount up for Bushong to play and sing his own compositions. Two were beautiful love songs, "The Girlfriend of a Boyfriend of Mine" and "One-Way Street." The other was a boogie-woogie parody entitled, "The Heat Is On." The message of "The Heat Is On" was that when the Texas Rangers forced gambling, prostitution and other forms of recreational sin out of Galveston, you could have appropriately "put a crepe on the old causeway."

Archie Crow and American National Insurance Co. agent Leroy Brown were very close friends. When they weren't at work, you rarely saw one without the other. Their wives, Lou Crow and Mildred "Shug" Brown were good friends, too.

As couples, they loved to ballroom dance, and there were plenty of places to do that. If Shep Fields and His Orchestra were playing at the Pleasure Pier's Marine Ballroom, for an example, you could depend on the Crows and the Browns being there. They never missed an annual Beta Sigma Phi "Ankles Away" production. Tell them there'd be dancing, the Crows and the Browns would be there for it.

Archie and Leroy were both Masons and Shriners. In fact, Archie was once the Potentate of Galveston's El Mina Shrine Temple. The Browns were members of Grace Episcopal Church, and before long the Crows were as well. The church records, in fact, show that Archie Crow was confirmed just before Christmas in 1955, by Bishop Godard of the Episcopal Diocese of Texas.

As the Crows got older, they began to long to move north of Huntsville. So when Archie sold his last Galveston restaurant and retired some years back, he and Lou moved to Trinity. The Browns remained in Galveston. Soon Shug Brown passed away. Some time later, Leroy married their longtime family friend, Carrie Jahn.

As frequently happens in friendships, changes of home location and changes of marital circumstances cause even the closest friendships to mellow into ones of memories and talks of old times. New shared events don't occur as frequently as they did in the past. Many times they dwindle down to where they rarely occur at all.

That was exactly where the Archie Crow-Leroy Brown friendship found itself about ten years ago. Contact became less and less frequent. Then Leroy Brown passed away, leaving his old friend, Archie Crow, behind. It was easy to think that event meant that the once close friendship of those two men could never be rekindled. Now it seems that having such thoughts may have been jumping to an invalid conclusion.

When Archie M. Crow, Jr. died, he was no longer an Episcopalian. He was a member of the Dorcas Wills Memorial Baptist Church in Trinity. And the pastor who presided at Archie Crow's funeral, the paper said, was the Rev. Leroy Brown.

Advertisement Galveston Isle Magazine

David Goodbar

The Rev. Max Brown was the pastor of First Baptist Church in the fall of 1989, and it was then that Franklin W. (Rusty) Carnes, III came to him with the news that he and his brother, Michael, had lost their jobs at a local funeral home.

The Carnes boys were third generation Galvestonians. Their grandfather Carnes had been with the Texas land grant office. Their father had managed the American National Insurance Co.'s mail room until a few years prior, when he passed away. There wasn't any question they were well-known and respected in the community, if for no other reason than their lineage.

Brown suggested that the Carnes boys should open their own funeral home. "That takes money," Rusty said, "And we don't have any."

David Goodbar was a deacon at First Baptist, and Brown had found that Goodbar had always been one of the church's most important problem-solving talents. "Go see David," Brown heard himself saying. "He'll figure out for you what to do."

It was at that same time that the real estate development business had taken its worse nose dive in nearly fifty years. Goodbar had been building a chain of motels, the Pelican Inns, when that happened. Almost overnight, that business had dried up.

And to make matters worse, because of the savings-and-loan and banking debacle, businesses were tightening their belts, and travel was suffering as a result. Goodbar's motels were in danger of failing as a result.

Sol Kotin had built for the A&P Food Store chain, a building at 23rd Street and Avenue K. Within the past couple of years, he had gotten it paid for by the rent. Now he was planning on that rental income providing a significant part of his retirement money. That was not to be. Kotin was in his seventies when he got notice that A&P would close its Galveston store and leave Kotin with a vacant 12,000-square-foot building.

Kotin knew he was now going to quickly need that building either leased or sold. After all property costs continue whether a building is used or not, and that property's insurance and taxes were placing a significant burden on Kotin's budget.

And there was a real-estate broker who had listed the property for sale or lease for Kotin, but he had gotten no bites. Like most other brokers at the time, he had seen his business go from making a lot of money each year, to making practically none.

When Rusty and Michael Carnes went to see Goodbar, he told them that if they and everyone they knew prayed, he might be able to do what seemed to be impossible—get them ownership of a new funeral home, get it for them even though they didn't have any significant finances of their own, and get them a large real-estate loan in a dried-up lending market.

By then Thanksgiving 1989 had passed. With Goodbar's sales assistance and his business expertise, the Carnes boys and Goodbar provided Henry Card with convincing evidence that he should loan the Carnes the money they would need for a down payment.

Card and the Carnes boys' father had, after all, been like brothers.

Next Goodbar used his own years of development expertise to analyze the available locations in town, and concluded that Kotin's property perfectly fit the criteria. It was centrally located, had sufficient off-street parking, met the space requirement, and because of the way it had been designed and built, would be easy to remodel and convert into a funeral home.

Goodbar was a master of the concept of networking. Tell enough people what you want, ask enough people if they know where you can get it, and eventually you'll get the answer you want. It was a laborious task, guaranteed to bring monumental "no's" just because of the times.

The final ingredient would be the hardest: finding a source for the loan. Goodbar felt it was ideal as a Small Business Administration Loan, but local banks were not interested, even with the government's guarantee on the note.

A friend told Goodbar that Ken Hutto, president of First National Bank of Missouri City, was aggressively building the value of his bank's portfolio and increasing profits by making SBA loans. Goodbar contacted Hutto, and within a month or so, the bank and the SBA agreed that the loan to the Carnes boys would fit the bank's portfolio. The loan was made.

On March 28, 1990, Sol Kotin sold his building, the real-estate broker earned a commission, Goodbar earned a consulting fee, the First National Bank of Missouri City made an SBA loan in Galveston, and the Carnes brothers had the foundation for their funeral home.

In less than five months, the A&P store was transformed into Carnes Brothers Funeral Home. Within recent months, Rusty and Mike Carnes' younger brother, Jay, joined the firm.

David Goodbar spent the last couple of years of his life in a predestined losing battle with Lou Gehrigs disease. It is a disease that progressively deteriorates all the muscles in your body but leaves the mind intact.

Many of those who knew David and his ability as a problem solver and negotiator, were never able to really accept that he wouldn't be the first person to recover from this disease. After all, when others were down-trodden, and David was, too, he predictably not only found a new way to slay the dragon for himself, but for his friends, too.

Two hundred fifty mourners from all walks of life and stretching every social strata in the county, joined together to hear his wife, Vikki, help them find resolution to their own personal loss of their friend, David, by her strong and revealing eulogy of the "Most Interesting Person She'd Ever Met," her husband of more than half of her life, David Goodbar.

Johnny's Part in a Class Act Comes to an End

When it comes to analyzing matters such as which was Galveston's finest supper club of a bygone era the Balinese Room usually wins out, but there are a substantial number of us who, when pressed, admit to being contrarians.

However, rather than start a hubbub, I had planned to keep that I am one of them to myself; that is, until I read in the paper that my friend Johnny Athanasiou died recently at seventy-seven.

So in honor of Johnny, let me just get this out in the open and over with. The most elegant club with the finest steaks that were ever cooked on this island comprised the signature of the Ricksha Room on Sixth Street, and it was owned by Johnny Athanasiou and his brothers, Diamond and Riley. If you never went there, I'm sorry. You would have loved it.

The Ricksha comprised the whole upstairs of the building, with a check-in desk and an electric door in a teeny downstairs lobby. After all, this was a time when selling liquor by the drink required sabotaging the efforts of the authorities, or paying them off—mostly both.

In the club there was a wonderful and intimate bar with a small dance floor adjacent to it, and just enough room for a combo. To the east was a plush dining room with tufted banquettes and shaded oil lamps on each white table-clothed table. You surmised Fred Astaire and Ginger Rogers were just running late. They would surely join the party at any moment.

Take a date there, and by evening's end she wanted to marry you, even if you were short, pimply faced, or just dorky because your family thought you were still to young to have tailor mades from Ace Tailors.

Now prior to the Ricksha, when 61st Street had charm, the Athanasiou boys had the Seabreeze Café, overlooking Offats Bayou. It was there that adults and teens danced on weekends to bands like Chano Rodriguez and the Realtoes; the Embers; Joe Biondo, Buzzy & Co.; and Danny Smith's group.

And it was there that Bubba Miller, now president and major stockholder of Interstate Batteries, impressed everyone including his date of the evening with his rendition of an extremely sexy dance called the bop.

Hurricane Carla and something named Progress together destroyed the Seabreeze and the charm of its neighboring water's edge bait camps and clapboard honky-tonks. The unbending force of Texas Attorney Will Wilson and his successors caused the demise of the Ricksha Room.

But on Saturday, December 20, 1997, as a Rotarian, I was ringing the bell for the Salvation Army at Wal-Mart. I had been there for more than forty-five minutes. Not one soul had put a thin dime in the kettle, yet perhaps a hundred people had gone by. Can you believe it?

Across the parking lot I saw Johnny get out of his car. As he started toward me, his hand went into his pocket and pulled out his wallet. He had heard the desperate ring of the Salvation Army bell, and he wouldn't pass that opportunity to help his fellow man. To do otherwise wouldn't be the Anthanasiou style.

"Thank you, and Merry Christmas, Mr. Athanasiou," I chimed as he put a wad of bills into the kettle. "The Ricksha was the best and I don't care who says otherwise," I added, always working that last thought into any conversation I had with him in later years.

But I ask you, how would I have known that would not only be his last Christmas, but my last opportunity to let him know that as far as many are concerned, the Ricksha was the best supper club Galveston ever had?

John Athanasiou

Frank Sinatra Should Have Picked Chano Rodriguez

Let's clear this up now. Frank Sinatra never heard Chano Rodriguez sing. If he had, Tony Bennett and Vic Damone couldn't claim Sinatra said each was the world's best crooner, because Sinatra wouldn't have said it about either of them, much less about both of them.

No, the evidence would have been just as empirical to Sinatra as it was to thousands upon thousands who heard Chano sing over the years: Any designation of "best crooner" belonged solely to Chano Rodriguez. Period. "End of conversation," Houstonian John W. Abbott said in agreement.

Let's take it another step farther. Had the world heard Chano's rendition of "La Bamba" before it heard Richie Valens', Valens wouldn't have been on the plane with the Big Bopper (Jiles Richardson) and Buddy Holly when it crashed just after midnight in snowy Clear Lake, Iowa, February 3, 1959, because "La Bamba" would have been Chano's song, not Valens'. And, after all, seventeen-year-old Valens didn't have but that one song.

My friend of nearly fifty years, Chano Rodriguez, fifty-eight, died of a heart attack, and a big part of the hearts of Galvestonians went to his grave with him. From his high school days in the mid-50s as Chano and the Rialtos, to his grown up days with the Johnny Garcia Trio, to his middle-aged days fronting Ronnie Ginsberg's group at the Bob Smith Yacht Club, Chano Rodriguez played a big part in kindling the romantic fires and keeping the embers burning of many Island couples of all ages. In fact, most didn't dream of celebrating any New Year's Eve much less a class reunion or wedding anniversary without Chano's serenades.

Always impeccably dressed and with beautiful manners ("A true gentleman," Vivian Renfro confirmed), that Rodriguez never made it to the top mystifies every single person who ever heard him sing, and every musician who ever backed him.

Paul Renfro, who played drums with Chano and the Rialtos, can still recall in his mind's ear walking down the hall at Lovenberg Jr. High School in 1954, and hearing Chano singing the "Ava Maria" solo in a choir classroom. "I get goose bumps when I think about it, just like I did then, and I didn't even know Chano at the time," Renfro muses.

My brother, Frederick Cherry, says Chano's voice had a sweetness to it, a very unusual quality, and he followed Chano's entire career beginning with his performances at Larry Kane's record hops in the 60s at the Pleasure Pier's Marine Room.

Often when Rodriguez was appearing, his wife Margaret, the only wife he ever had, would sit alone at a table for two. It was obvious to everyone, including her, that she wasn't really alone, because Chano sang every one of the romantic ballads to her. He would join her during the breaks. They would hold hands, and she would get his undivided attention. And then sometime during the night he would leave the bandstand, go to her table and ask her for a dance. The floor would become theirs, and theirs alone. The whole thing from start to finish had to have been the inspiration for that obligatory scene in every musical you've ever seen.

Once Chano and wonderful jazz pianist Johnny Garcia, along with bassist Oscar Garcia, decided to see if Las Vegas would give them their star. Temporarily leaving their families behind, they booked in as a lounge show, but it wasn't long before Chano knew he needed to be with Margaret, and Johnny knew he needed to be with his wife, Melba. Vegas wasn't a place to raise a family anyway, they decided, so they came back to Galveston.

By now gigs for musicians here weren't easy to find, for after all, nightly entertainment in Galveston nightclubs had gone away, side by side with the city's gambling casinos. So Chano resorted to a most incongrous job for him, driving a Yellow Cab. He performed on weekends.

It was only a short time later that the Flagship Hotel, which was new, began floundering under its first management, so the owner, Houstonian Jimmy Lyons, hired Jack Bushong from the Jack Tar Grand Bahamas Hotel to save the Flagship from financial ruin.

A part of the Bushong success formula was to book the Johnny Garcia Trio Plus One—Johnny, Chano, Oscar, and young singer Kathryn McDonald—as the every night entertainment package for the hotel restaurant and bar. We're talking about the mid-60s.

Galveston Memories

A number of years later with yet another big win under his belt, Bushong would consider retirement, and all who worked for him knew that without him, things would not be the same. Johnny and Melba Garcia decided to move to California where there was work for musicians; Kathryn McDonald had married and moved away; and Oscar Garcia was having health problems and needed time off.

This time Chano got a day job as a warrant officer, and resumed his "singing-when- one-night-gigs-are-available" career, performing on weekends, holidays and other occasions. That's how it was for the remainder of his life.

At about six p.m. one evening, Chano went to Lowe's in Texas City. On his way back home he had a fatal heart attack as he was driving. On the following Saturday morning Palmer Highway and the northbound lanes of the Gulf Freeway came to almost total standstills as the enormous funeral procession accompanied Chano from the church to the cemetery. More than one person has told me it was the largest funeral procession they had ever seen. People by the hundreds who were not in the procession pulled off the road and stopped. Many got out of their cars and bowed their heads to show reverence as Chano's hearse passed.

Chano sang this verse of "La Bamba" many times: "*Para subir al cielo. Para subir al cielo, se necesita una escalera grande . . . ,*" which translates, "To go up to heaven, to go up to heaven, you need a big ladder...." Chano had a big ladder. It was his voice.

I'm confident that there is a positive end to this story. Now Sinatra will finally hear Chano sing, and he'll get the long overdue message to Bennett and Damone, putting them on notice that the chairman of the board made an unfortunate mistake: Neither of them is the best crooner after all; it's a gentleman from Galveston, Texas, he's just met named Chano Rodriguez.

Chano Rodriguez